Exploring Christianity

DR. HENRY G. COVERT

Exploring Christianity
by Dr. Henry G. Covert

Copyright © 2023
All rights reserved.

The Scripture texts used in this publication are from the New International Version of the Holy Bible, published by Zondervan Bible Publishers, Grand Rapids, Michigan.

Library of Congress Control Number: 2023933666
International Standard Book Number: 978-1-60126-849-5

Masthof Press
219 Mill Road | Morgantown, PA 19543-9516
www.Masthof.com

Table of Contents

Acknowledgments v

Introduction vii

Chapter One: *Church Doctrine* 1

Chapter Two: *Crucifixion of Jesus* 71

Chapter Three: *Christian Life and Ministry* 115

Chapter Four: *The True Church* 149

Resources 170

Acknowledgments

This book is dedicated to everyone who seeks to find meaning and fulfillment in their Christian journey. It was written to provide spiritual insights that will ignite a new spark of hope for Christian living and ministry.

To my wife Katherine, who has always encouraged me and supported my ministries.

Introduction

Like the parable of the *Prodigal Son,* I had traveled far from the Father's house; however, because of my early Christian foundation I knew that there was hope in Jesus Christ. Parents are given the responsibility of planting the seeds of our Savior's teachings, as well as being spiritual guides and examples for their children. I rejoice and give thanks that my parents kept their promise to the Lord.

In this book I provide a succinct overview that highlights interpretations that most Christians share. A book could be written for each topic given; therefore, the subjects are only a starting point to stimulate thought and to encourage further examination and study. Recognizing that some churches have in-depth writings on the sacraments and doctrine, I have tried to tread lightly in this area.

In my analysis of the Church, I focus upon the areas that need change, especially if the Church is to meet spiritual and practical needs. The objective for all congregations is an outreach that speaks to people where they are in life, offering biblical and realistic ministry. This section also makes us realize the importance of developing a spiritual life outside the structure of the Church. Community churches should always be a guide that encourages spiritual formation through personal devotion, prayer, and study.

Although this writing is brief, it has been a challenge to examine Christian doctrine and ministry. As I walk on sacred ground, I am aware that my words will be scrutinized by people from all denominations and faith persuasions. My intentions are not to judge any Christian group or church, but rather to bring us to a place of self-examination for the purpose of positive change and spiritual formation. It is to challenge our faith, traditions and ministries, for the purpose of maximizing our personal potential and ministry to others. We live in a fast-moving and complex world where our emotions are put to the test, and little time is given to matters of the soul. The Church sometimes reflects the secular world, which means that we often approach worship and ministry in a mechanical way that simply becomes part of our busy schedule. This is one reason why we must prayerfully nurture the inner life apart from structured Christianity.

— CHAPTER ONE —

Church Doctrine

CREATION AND SIN

The prophet Isaiah wrote, "All of us have become like one who is unclean, and all our righteous acts are like filthy rags; we all shrivel up like a leaf, and like the wind, our sins sweep us away." (Isaiah 64:6) Saint Paul told the Christians in Rome that "all have sinned and fall short of the glory of God." (Romans 3:23) Likewise, the apostle John wrote, "If we claim to be without sin, we deceive ourselves, and the truth is not in us. If we claim we have not sinned, we make him out to be a liar, and his word has no place in our lives." (I John 1:8-10)

    The Bible provides us with the creation story, the introduction of sin, and humanity's fall from grace that resulted from pride and disobedience. The Genesis account reveals that God created the first man and woman out of love and in His image. Their holy and sinless state enabled them to be in perfect union with their Creator. Like the Godhead, they had distinct personalities, experienced feelings and emotions, and exercised free will. The Lord provided for all of their needs, and they were told to increase in number. God gave them every seed-bearing plant, as well as the authority over every living creature. (Genesis 1:26-31) The free will that was given to them is significant, for it enabled them to love God and one another.

Prior to God creating humanity, there were angels living in the heavenly realm. (Job 38:6-7; Hebrews 12:22) The Scriptures speak of different classes of angels who served God in various ways. Paul alluded to the creation of angels, and the writer of Hebrews informs us of their ministering functions. (Colossians 1:16; Hebrews 1:14) King David mentions the created order of angels, and the apostle Peter speaks about their power. (Psalm 8:4-5; II Peter 2:11) However, it is Ezekiel who reveals a guardian cherub who was cast out of heaven because of his wickedness. This angel, known to the Christian Church as Satan or the devil, developed an unrighteous pride that corrupted his wisdom. (Ezekiel 28:11-17) The Bible states that Satan's fall from grace also involved other angels who followed his sinful path. (Job 4:18-19; Matthew 25:41; II Peter 2:4; Jude 6; Revelation 12:3-9) The prophet Isaiah wrote about the devil's pride, revealing his desire to be like God and have our Creator's glory. (Isaiah 14:12-14)

It is Satan who caused the first man and woman to sin. Regardless which one sinned first, both the man and woman were caught in Satan's trap. Disguised as a serpent, Satan planted doubt in their minds, which led them to sin against God. The devil questioned God's command that Adam and Eve not eat or touch the fruit from a particular tree that was in the center of the Garden of Eden. In opposition to what God said, Satan told them that they would not die if they ate from the tree. In fact, the devil assured them that by eating the fruit they would become like God, knowing good and evil. (Genesis 3:1-5) Adam and Eve allowed pride to consume them, and they submitted to the temptation and lost God's grace. From that day, life became a struggle for them and their offspring. Although the Lord still loved them, they had to live with the results of their sin. They lost their holiness and innocence, realized their nakedness without God and, losing their innocence, they became aware of good and evil in the world. Physical death also became a reality, for their days on earth were numbered and, without repentance and reconciliation with God, there would be spiritual death.

Some individuals and Christian groups not only dispute the creation story, but they also question the existence of Satan. They believe that the words *Adam* and *Eve* are simply gender references. While this may be true, it does not negate the Lord's creation of the first man and woman and the truths found in the biblical story. Those who refute the reality of the devil believe that the word *Satan* is only a symbol to express evil. These individuals disregard the numerous references to Satan that are found in both the Hebrew Bible and the New Testament. As such, it is important that we examine the Scriptures that support the reality of Satan.

The existence of Satan is found in seven Old Testament books and affirmed by every New Testament writer. Jesus acknowledged the presence of Satan in our world, emphasizing his evil and destructive power. He told his disciples that the devil sows seeds that lead people into sin and rebellion. (Matthew 13:39) When followers of Jesus informed Him of the miracles that they performed in His name, He said to them, "I saw Satan fall like lightning from heaven." (Luke 10:18) During His earthly ministry, Jesus repeatedly referred to Satan and the reality of demon possession. Paul wrote the Ephesians that "our struggle is not against flesh and blood, but against the rulers, against the authorities, against the powers of this dark world and against the spiritual forces of evil in the heavenly realms." (Ephesians 6:12) This statement refers to Satan and the fallen angels who followed him into sin.

The translation of the word *Satan* is adversary, and the word *devil* is understood as slanderer. While these terms are familiar to us, the New Testament writers offer other descriptive words for the devil. The apostle John called Satan the prince of this world, the evil one, great dragon and the accuser. (John 12:31; I John 5:19; Revelation 12:1-10) In Matthew we find the word *Beelzebub*, which means the prince of demons. (Matthew 12:24) In referring to Satan, Paul called him the god of this age, *Belial* (personification of evil), the angel of light, and ruler of the kingdom of the air. (II Corinthians 4:4; 6:15; 11:14; Ephesians 2:2) The Scriptures leave no doubt about the reality of Satan and his intentions, and those who reject these biblical references have succumbed to his deceit. Satan's most effective weapon is convincing people that he does not exist.

In his foreknowledge, God knew that evil would enter our lives. Immediately after the fall of humanity we find Messianic passages that point to the battle between good and evil, including prophetic words relating to the crucifixion of Jesus. (Genesis 3:15; Isaiah 53) We must conclude that an omniscient God knew the future before He created humanity. This, of course, raises a question. If God knew that humanity would sin, then why did He create man and woman? The answer to this question may be found in our own lives. For example, why do married couples desire children when they know beforehand that they will be born into sin? What parent has not experienced the sins of their children? So, why are people intent upon having offspring?

Some people speak about their desire to continue the family name or the need to create an extension of themselves. Children share our genes and characteristics; therefore, in a sense they are created in our image, for better or worse. These are certainly motivators to desire children. However, the underlying reason that most people want children relates to parental love. We create offspring in order to share our lives with them, believing that our participation in a child's development can produce positive results. Even though we know that there will be difficult times, our willingness is rooted in love and hope. Although we cannot know God's wisdom, this analogy seems plausible.

Because the Lord knew that sin would enter His creation, He prepared in advance for our forgiveness and salvation. Before the earthly life of Jesus, humanity was expected to respond to their guilt through repentance and prayer. God gave His people the law and a system of sacrifices that were intended to open their minds and hearts to the existence of sin and the need for forgiveness. But Jesus Christ has fulfilled the law through His love and sacrificial death. In Christ there is one atoning sacrifice for all people, past, present and future. In Jesus, we have a Savior who has lived our life and knows our struggles with temptation and sin. His identification with humanity arouses His compassion and power, providing the grace to keep us strong.

God created us out of love, with the desire to share His life and creation with us. It is because of this love that He is willing to suffer through our sins, knowing that His grace can transform us. The Lord is willing to bury our past and give us a new beginning and future. (Hebrews 8:12) The gift of forgiveness and salvation is free, but we must reach out and accept it through repentance and faith in Jesus Christ. Jesus told a story about a shepherd who left his flock to go after one lost sheep. This is God's story, for every life is precious in His sight. I firmly believe that Christ would have given His life for just one lost sinner. Yes, even though God knew that we would sin, He was willing to give His most precious gift, His only begotten Son, that we might be saved.

THE NATURE AND LIFE OF JESUS
Humanity of Jesus

It would be difficult to dispute the human nature of Jesus, given the fact that He experienced all the emotions, physical needs, and the pain of humanity. Even His crucifixion, although prophesied for our forgiveness and salvation, reveals a human death. Jesus was born of a woman (Luke 2:1-7; Galatians 4:4), subject to human development (Luke 2:21-52), had physical needs (Matthew 4:2; John 19:28), experienced limitations (John 4:6), and His compassion led to tears (John 11:35). He was also tempted and confronted with every manner of evil. (Luke 4:1-13; Hebrews 2:18; 4:15) We even learn of our Savior's anger over the people's disrespect for the temple in Jerusalem. Although it was a righteous anger, Jesus shouted at those who were selling items for profit, and He turned over the tables of the money changers. (Mark 11:15-19; John 2:13-17)

As the Son of Man, Jesus knows how it feels to be lonely, rejected, misunderstood, ridiculed by others, persecuted, physically tortured and put to death. Although He was sinless, His descent into hell enabled Him to experience the eternal reality of unrepentant sinners. He knows both the pain of the body and the agony of the soul, and He will eternally carry the scars of humanity. In Jesus Christ we have a Savior who walks with us and whose Spirit lives within us. Regardless what trial we may face in this life, He has gone before us, paving the way for God's mercy and sustaining grace.

Divinity of Jesus

The divine nature of Jesus is repeatedly confirmed in New Testament writings. The apostle John, whom many scholars believe had a special relationship with our Savior, calls Jesus the Logos, which means the Word of God. John emphasizes Jesus' divinity with the following words:

> In the beginning was the Word, and the Word was with God, and the Word was God. He was with God in the beginning. Through him all things were made; without him nothing was made that has been made. In him was life, and that life was the light of men. The light shines in the darkness, but the darkness has not understood it. The Word became flesh and lived for a while among us. We have seen his glory, the glory of the one and only Son, who came down

from the Father, full of grace and truth. No one has ever seen God, but God the only Son, who is at the Father's side. (John 1:1-5, 14-18)

John the Baptist was called by God to prepare the way for Jesus' message of forgiveness and salvation. He told the people that someone would come after him, whose sandals he was unworthy to untie. John's ministry was to make people aware of their sins and thus the need for the Lord's forgiving grace. The Jews were expecting a Messiah, but they were looking for a political figure to release them from their Roman overlords and restore their spiritual and cultural dignity. John the Baptist, by encouraging people to examine their hearts, was pointing them to a Savior who would give them spiritual and eternal life.

Jesus entered this world through the mystery of divine intervention. The angel Gabriel announced to Mary that she would give birth to a male child, whom she was to name Jesus. Mary was told that her child would be called the Son of the Most High. When Mary questioned the angel, she learned that the conception would be accomplished through the power of the Holy Spirit. (Luke 1:26-38) The *Virgin Birth* of Jesus has traditionally been accepted by the Church and has been incorporated into Christian dogma and creeds. In the Roman Catholic Church this doctrine is known as the *Immaculate Conception*, meaning that Mary was free of original sin at the moment of conception. Other faith groups, while believing in the *Virgin Birth*, do not make this statement

The events surrounding the birth of Jesus also reveal His divinity. Luke informs us that an angel of the Lord appeared to shepherds who were living in a field near Bethlehem. The angel announced the birth of Jesus, saying, "Today in the town of David a Savior has been born to you; he is Christ the Lord." After this glorious announcement, there appeared a great company of heavenly host who echoed, "Glory to God in the highest, and on earth peace to men on whom his favor rests." (Luke 2:8-14) This message to the shepherds announced a divine birth that would physically unite God with humanity. It was a birth that would bring hope to a lost and dying world.

The visit of the Magi also speaks to the significance of our Lord's birth. We learn that these men traveled to Jerusalem from a location in the east. Upon their arrival they asked, "Where is the one who has been born king of the Jews? We have seen his star in the east and have come to worship him." (Matthew 2:1-2) The word *worship* is noteworthy, for the Magi apparently believed that the birth of Jesus had spiritual importance. In the Hebrew Bible the word *magi* was used for priests and wise men who lived among the Medes, Persians and Babylonians. They were thought to be astronomers and astrologers, who searched for higher knowledge and truth. The early Church believed that these particular Magi may have been the first worshippers of Christ. An understanding that the Jewish Messiah was to rule the world, may have led these men to the Jewish capital.

The life and ministry of Jesus continuously manifested His divinity to the people, particularly to His apostles who lived with Him for approximately three years. Jesus told them that all authority in heaven and on earth was given to Him by the Father. (Matthew 28:18) His divine character was manifested in His thoughts, words and actions, all of which have been given to us by witnesses and inspired writers. Prior to His arrest and execution, He performed many miracles, some of which are recorded in the Scriptures. After calling His first disciples He traveled through Galilee, where He taught in the synagogues and preached the good news of God's kingdom. In these and other travels He healed every manner of sickness and disease. As the news about Him continued to spread throughout the region, people were coming to Him from great distances.

According to Matthew, Jesus healed everyone who came to Him. (Matthew 4:23-25) On one evening in the town of Capernaum, He was overwhelmed with sick people, some of whom were carried to Him by family members and friends. Whether it was in the villages, towns or countryside, the sick were placed before Him. The crowds begged Jesus to allow them to touch Him, believing that this alone would make them well. It is reported that such healings did occur. (Matthew 9:18; Mark 1:32-34; 6:53-56; Luke 4:38-44)

One multiple healing involved ten lepers who stood at the entrance of a village, crying out to Jesus for mercy. Having learned of His compassion and power, they desperately called out to Him as He approached the village. But, instead of touching the lepers, Jesus tested their faith. He told them to go to the priests for the certification of their healing, which would allow them to return to society. Since leprosy was thought to be associated with a spiritual problem, the lepers were required to be examined by the priests. While en route, all ten men were completely healed of their dreadful disease. Unfortunately, however, only one returned to give Jesus thanks and praise. (Luke 17:11-19)

Like the lepers whom Jesus healed, He restored sight to the blind and hearing to the deaf. (Matthew 9:27-31; 20:29-34; Mark 7:31-37; 8:22-25; 10:46-52; John 9:1-12) With some of the healings, the Pharisees and other religious leaders tried to investigate in an attempt to discredit Jesus. (John 9:13-34) Needless to say, they walked away in a state of confusion. The mention of these investigations is important, for they substantiate the validity of the miracles. In an attempt to bolster their own authority, the religious elite continuously voiced their rejection of Jesus to the people.

The apostles tell us that many paralytics were brought to Jesus, some of whom were disabled from birth. On one of His visits to Capernaum, a Roman centurion asked Jesus to restore his paralyzed servant who was experiencing severe pain. Jesus offered to go to the centurion's home, but the officer said to Him, "Lord, I do not deserve to have you come under my roof. But just say the word and my servant will be healed." Can you imagine a high-ranking Roman officer addressing Jesus in this manner? We must not forget that the Jews were living under Roman occupation. This interaction would not have occurred if the centurion did not believe in Jesus' divine power. In response to the officer, Jesus said, "I tell you the truth, I have not found anyone in Israel with such faith. Go! It will be done just as you believed it would." According to Matthew, the centurion's servant was immediately healed. (Matthew 8:5-13; cp. Mark 2:1-12; Luke 5:17-26)

Delivering individuals from evil spirits was another sign of Jesus' ministry; however, there are theologians today who reject the notion of demonic possession. They claim that the biblical accounts reflect individuals who suffered from epilepsy or another disease that caused convulsions or seizures. If this is true, why did Jesus refer to these cases as demonic possessions? How could the Son of God not know a disease from an evil possession? In fact, the Scriptures make a distinction between such diseases and possessions. (Matthew 4:24) Also, when we read the accounts of Jesus expelling demons, we are told of the multiple voices and the statements made by the demons. In fact, their responses revealed fear when Jesus confronted them. (Mark 1:21-28) In one case, after Jesus expelled demons from an individual, they entered swine that were nearby. It is recorded that the possessed herd ran down a steep bank into a lake and died. (Matthew 8:28-34; Luke 8:26-39)

Although I had some experience with demonic possession early in my ministry, I came in direct contact with this evil while serving as a state prison chaplain. There is a stark difference between people who choose a criminal lifestyle and those who are possessed with evil. Their desires, words, voice reflections, body language and actions, have eliminated any doubt in my mind. There was also no doubt in the minds of Jesus and His apostles. It is a chilling experience to be in the presence of demonic possession.

We know that our Savior healed every sickness and disease, but His greatest power was revealed when He raised the dead. In the city of Nain, which was about ten miles from Nazareth, Jesus restored life to a dead man. Out of compassion for the man's mother, He touched the coffin that was being carried, telling the man to rise. The man immediately sat up and began to speak. The people were filled with awe and praised God, saying, "A great prophet has appeared among us. God has come to help his people." (Luke 7:11-17) Jesus also raised the twelve-year-old daughter of a synagogue ruler. He took the little girl by the hand and told her to rise. When her spirit returned to her body, Jesus told the parents to give her something to eat. (Matthew 9:18-19, 23-26; Mark 5:21-24, 35-43; Luke 8:40-56)

The raising of Lazarus from the dead reveals some interesting facts. Jesus had a special relationship with Lazarus and his sisters, Martha and Mary. He often visited their home when He was in or near Bethany. But when Jesus heard that Lazarus was seriously ill and near death, He did not immediately respond. Instead, He stayed where He was for two more days. This seemed strange, knowing how close He was with the family. However, Jesus knew that Lazarus was going to die, and His delay was intended to bring joy to the family and glory to God. When Jesus arrived in Bethany, Lazarus had already been in the tomb for four days, and his body was beginning to deteriorate. In fact, Martha reminded Jesus of this, telling him that the body was in a state of decay and stench. Jesus responded by telling Martha to believe in Him. When the entrance stone of the sepulcher was removed, Jesus called Lazarus to rise and come out of the tomb. Although Lazarus was bound in wrappings, he was able to obey Jesus' command. When Martha saw this, she knew that Jesus was the Son of God. (John 11:17-44)

Jesus' power to heal the sick and raise the dead were miracles that laid the foundations of faith for many witnesses. In Jesus they knew that God had entered their world. Some people even saw our Savior's power over nature, and His ability to feed thousands of people with only enough food for a few individuals. While in a boat on the Sea of Galilee, the apostles were astonished as their

Master took command of swirling winds and turbulent waters. In fear and amazement, they asked one another, "Who is this? He commands the wind and the water, and they obey him." (Matthew 8:23-27; Mark 4:35-41; Luke 8:22-25) One day the apostles saw Jesus leave the shoreline and walk on the sea toward them. They were terrified, believing that they were observing a ghost. (Mark 6:45-52)

A miracle that directly involved the apostles was the feeding of five thousand people with just two fish and five loaves of bread. Thousands of people had followed Jesus to a remote area, where they listened to Him teaching about the kingdom of God. Because it was getting late, the apostles wanted Jesus to dismiss the crowd, thus enabling them to go to the nearby villages for food. But Jesus told His apostles that they should feed the people. They were shocked, for they barely had enough food to feed themselves. Jesus then took the two fish and five loaves of bread that the apostles had, offered up prayer, and miraculously fed the five thousand people. The food kept multiplying, and there was even a small amount left over. (Mark 6:30-44; 8:1-13; John 6:1-15) This is one of two recorded miracles in which Jesus fed thousands of people.

Peter, James and John, witnessed another display of Jesus' divinity. At our Savior's invitation, they accompanied Him to the top of a mountain for prayer. As Jesus was praying, the apostles saw His appearance change and His clothing become intensely bright. When this happened, Moses and Elijah appeared in glorious splendor. They spoke to Jesus about His imminent death and return to glory. After this conversation, a cloud came over the mountain, and a voice from the cloud said, "This is my Son, whom I love; with him I am well pleased. Listen to him!" (Matthew 17:1-8; Mark 9:2-8; Luke 9:28-36) These three apostles became leaders of the Church, with this experience strengthening their faith and commitment. Jesus knew that they needed unwavering faith if they were to preach the Gospel in the midst of adversity and persecution.

We cannot speak about the divinity of Jesus without providing some insight into His omniscient nature. New Testament writers provide many instances when Jesus knew both the thoughts of people and future events. He spoke about His death and how long He would be in the grave before His resurrection. (Mark 10:32-34) He predicted Judas' betrayal, saying that one of the twelve apostles would falsely accuse Him before the religious authorities. (Mark 14:17-21; Luke 22:21-22; John 13:21-30) Jesus also knew that Peter would deny knowing Him. He said to Peter, "I tell you the truth, this very night, before the rooster crows, you will disown me three times." This came true after Jesus was arrested, and Peter wept bitterly. (Matthew 26:33-34, 69-75; Mark 14:66-72; Luke 22:54-62) But Peter was not the only apostle to shield himself from danger, for Jesus knew that His crucifixion would put fear into the hearts of the other disciples. He said to them, "You will all fall away on account of me, for it is written, 'I will strike the shepherd, and the sheep of the flock will be scattered.'" (Zechariah 13:7; Matthew 26:31; Mark 14:27)

Jesus prophesied the persecution of the Jews by the Roman army, as well as the destruction of the temple in Jerusalem. (Matthew 24:1-2; Mark 13:1-2) He also had knowledge of the events that will precede His Second Advent. While these things have not yet occurred, we can be certain of their future reality. We anxiously await our Lord's victorious return, when He will appear in all His glory to judge the world and usher in God's eternal kingdom. While some people question this promise, believing that Jesus was probably speaking in abstract terms or spiritualizing His return, His graphic words leave no room for doubt. We must also remember that God's perception of time is far different from our understanding. Peter spoke about this when people doubted the promise of Jesus' return. (II Peter 3:8-9)

Two passages of scripture that are often overlooked when examining Jesus' supernatural gifts relate to the calling of Nathanael, and Jesus' ability to help His apostles with their fishing difficulties. These events may seem insignificant in comparison to His other miracles, but they were certainly important to those involved. Nathanael, who could not imagine God's Messiah coming from the town of Nazareth, learned that Jesus was no ordinary man. When he was asked to meet Jesus, he discovered that our Savior has unusual vision. Jesus saw Nathanael before he was visually in our Lord's sight. When Nathanael realized this, he became an instant believer. He said to Jesus, "Rabbi, you are the Son of God; you are the King of Israel." (John 1:43-49) There were two other occasions when Jesus revealed His supernatural vision. They were times when the apostles had been fishing for many hours and could not locate any fish. Jesus directed them to locations where the fish were plentiful and, after following His instructions, their nets were so full that they began to tear apart. (Luke 5:1-10; John 21:1-11) According to the apostle John, Jesus performed numerous miracles that are not recorded in the Scriptures. (John 21:25)

Jesus' Power Given to the Apostles

The Scriptures inform us that Jesus gave certain powers to His apostles. They were given the authority to drive out demons, to heal every sickness and disease and, in some cases, to raise the dead. (Matthew 10:1; Luke 9:1-6) In addition to the apostles, Jesus sent out seventy-two other disciples, telling them to visit every town and place where He was about to go. He said, "Heal the sick that are there, and tell them that the kingdom of God is near." Upon returning, they informed Jesus of the mighty works that were done in His name. (Luke 10:1-17) In the book of Acts we learn that the apostles performed many miraculous signs and wonders that increased the number of believers. People brought all their sick to the apostles, carrying many of them on beds and mats. Some people believed that they would be healed by simply being in the proximity of the apostle Peter. (Acts 5:12-16)

Peter is credited with healing a crippled beggar who sat at the gate to the temple. The man was lame since birth, and he was carried to the gate to solicit alms from those entering the temple. Peter gave the man a gift far greater than money. In Jesus' name, he healed the paralytic. (Acts 3:1-10) Also, when he was in the town of Lydda, Peter healed a paralytic who had been bedridden for eight years. (Acts 9:32-35) While in Lydda, he was informed that a woman named Tabitha had just died in nearby Joppa. She was a believer and a servant to the poor. Peter was urged to visit the room where her body was placed. When he arrived, he knelt down to pray near the dead woman. He then told Tabitha to get up. She opened her eyes, and Peter helped her to her feet. (Acts 9:32-43) During a trip to Israel I visited Joppa, and I went to the location where Peter stayed after he performed this miracle. It was at the home of a man named Simon, who was a tanner in that town. Although the house no longer exists, the foundation of the property is still in place. It was a strange feeling to be standing where Peter lodged after this glorious event.

Paul had his own encounter with someone who had died. It was while he was speaking to a group of people in Troas. He was addressing a large crowd that had gathered in a third-floor room and, as the hours passed by, the people were becoming exhausted. Around midnight, a young man named Eutychus fell three stories from a windowsill where he was sitting. It is reported that he died from the fall, but Paul threw himself on the man and placed his arms around him. This action, which had some type of spiritual significance, brought the man back to life. This comforted the crowd, giving them the assurance of Paul's anointing and his calling to preach the Gospel. (Acts 20:7-12)

The miracles performed by the apostles are mentioned because their power was given to them by Jesus. These spiritual gifts could only be given by God, proving that in Jesus Christ there is power over life and death. The apostles realized that the presence of the Almighty was in Jesus, and that it was only through Him that they could heal the sick, expel demons and raise the dead. This power was instrumental in spreading the Gospel and leading people to Christ. Today, caution must be taken when someone claims to have these powers. I have seen people's lives destroyed by those who profess to be healers, or claim to have some other miraculous power. Healing lies within the will of God, and we are called to trust in His wisdom. We should also remember that life is eternal, which means that death is the ultimate healer.

Jesus Before the Authorities

At the end of His ministry Jesus was arrested and taken before the Sanhedrin, which was the Jewish Council. This appearance provides additional insight into His divinity and mission. The members of the Sanhedrin were seeking evidence that would warrant Jesus' death. Since the Jews were under Roman authority, they were not permitted to execute anyone. They could, however, refer someone to the Roman government if the charge was of a treasonous nature. After intense questioning, the high priest asked Jesus, "Are you the Christ, the Son of the Blessed One?" Jesus answered, "I am, and you will see the Son of Man sitting at the right hand of the Mighty One, and coming on the clouds of heaven." (Mark 14:53-65) Although the Sanhedrin saw this as blasphemy, they knew that the Roman government would not execute someone on this charge.

The morning after Jesus was questioned by the Jewish Council, the chief priests, elders, and teachers of the law, made a decision. They bound Jesus and took Him to Pontius Pilate, who was the Roman procurator of Judea. Pilate was unconcerned about the Jewish religion and the charges that the Jews placed against Jesus. He believed that the religious leaders were jealous of Jesus and had ulterior motives for their actions. To confront Pilate's lack of concern, the religious authorities told him that Jesus claimed to be a king, and that he was inciting the people and causing disruption wherever he went. If this were true, it could be considered treason, for Caesar was the sole ruler of the Roman Empire.

Pilate resisted charging Jesus, believing that He was an innocent man. Pilate's wife even had a dream about Jesus, which she conveyed to her husband. In her uneasiness, she told Pilate not to have anything to do with Him. Eventually, Pilate asked Jesus if He was the king of the Jews, and He responded by saying that His kingdom was not an earthly one. He said, "My kingdom is not of this world. If it were, my servants would fight to prevent my arrest by the Jews. But now my kingdom is from another place. I came into the world to testify to the truth. Everyone on the side of truth listens to me." (John 18:36-37)

After pressure from the Jewish leaders, Pilate finally agreed to sentence Jesus to death. This was done to appease the Sanhedrin, for Pilate did not want them telling the authorities in Rome that he refused to sentence a Jew who was guilty of treason. Jesus was held for execution, while another prisoner named Barabbas was set free. Barabbas was in prison with insurrectionists, who had committed murder in an uprising against Roman authority. Each year during the Passover holiday, a prisoner was set free by the Roman government. Passover, which commemorated the exodus of the Jews from Egypt, was a tense time because the Jews anticipated that their Messiah would come during this holiday. To ease the tension, the government set a policy to release one prisoner each year during this celebration. (Matthew 27:11-26; Mark 15:1-15)

The Atoning Death of Jesus

The crucifixion of Jesus was a contradiction to the Messianic beliefs of the Jews. After all, how could God's Messiah submit to Roman authority and be executed. But the atoning sacrifice of Jesus was foretold in the Hebrew Scriptures. (Genesis 3:15; Isaiah 53; Psalm 22:1) In the New Testament, Jesus' death is mentioned at least 175 times, which speaks to its significance within the providence of God. Jesus said that He came to give His life as a ransom. (Matthew 20:28; I Timothy 2:6) The writer of Hebrews restated this truth when he wrote that "the death of Jesus has taken away the devil's power of death over us." (Hebrews 2:14) This statement relates to spiritual death and the loss of salvation. To receive the blessings of our Lord's sacrifice is to be forgiven and empowered to walk in the Spirit. Paul tells us that the crucifixion of Jesus lies at the heart of the Gospel. He wrote that Christ died for our sins according to the Scriptures. (I Corinthians 15:1-3)

The events that took place during the crucifixion are noteworthy. Most victims of crucifixion remained alive for several days or longer, undergoing the torture of body cramps, dehydration and asphyxiation. This is not to mention the pain associated with festering wounds and infection. There was also suffering related to weather conditions and animals that saw the victims as prey. Crucifixion was the most agonizing and degrading means of punishment and death. For the Jew, it was also considered a curse. In Deuteronomy we read, "If a man guilty of a capital offense is put to death and his body is hung on a tree, you must not leave his body on the tree overnight. Be sure to bury him the same day, because anyone who is hung on a tree is under God's curse." (Deuteronomy 21:22-23) The Jewish law stated that once a person was dead, justice was served. To expose a corpse beyond the pronouncement of death defiled the land and was a public disgrace. Although this understanding did not relate to the circumstances surrounding Jesus' death, the Jews probably applied this scripture to all executions.

Jesus was only on the cross a matter of hours when He cried out, "It is finished." He then voluntarily yielded up His spirit to the Father and died. Some theologians believe that the unusual rapidity of the Lord's death may have resulted from the brutal beatings that He endured prior to the execution. While this may be true, it remains that He willingly gave up His life. When speaking to religious leaders during His ministry, Jesus spoke about His imminent death. He said, "I lay down my life for the sheep. The reason my Father loves me is that I lay down my life – only to take it up again. No one takes it from me, but I lay it down of my own accord. I have authority to lay it down and the authority to take it up again. This command I received from my Father." (John 10:15-18) The divine nature of Christ is clearly communicated in this statement.

When Jesus died, the light of day turned to darkness. This was followed by an earthquake that split rocks and opened tombs. We are told that the bodies of saints who had died were brought back to life. We cannot be certain, but these individuals may have been resurrected to be witnesses of Jesus' divinity and His power over death. (Matthew 27:45-56) Upon Jesus' death, the veil in the Jerusalem temple was torn in two from top to bottom. This curtain separated the inner sanctuary of the Holy of Holies from the rest of the temple. The Holy of Holies was reserved for the intercessory functions of the priest. The severing of this curtain was an act of God, disclosing that priestly intercession had come to an end. The way to the Father was now through God's Son. Jesus had previously told His disciples that no one comes to the Father except through Him. (Matthew 27:50-51; John 14:6)

With our limited knowledge and understanding it is impossible to know the mysteries of God, and this includes the spiritual depth of the crucifixion. But we are certain that Jesus gave His life as an atoning sacrifice for our forgiveness and salvation. The Father knew that the mission of His Son would result in His death, and He made this the door to eternal life in His kingdom. Those who receive Jesus and His sacrifice for humanity are reconciled with the Father. The penalty for sin that we justly deserve was borne by Jesus, for only God was able to do what is impossible for us. In Chapter Two we will discuss the crucifixion in more detail.

Anticipating his death, Jesus asked the Father if the cup of suffering could be taken from Him. But His prayer was for the Father's will, which led him to the cross. This unconditional love is difficult for us to comprehend, especially when it is God who was willing to endure such agonizing pain for rebellious sinners. (Matthew 26:39) The apostles knew that Jesus had predicted His death, and they were troubled by His words. In fact, it angered Peter to hear his Master talk about being crucified. He once rebuked Jesus, saying, "Never, Lord! This shall never happen to you." But our Savior said to Peter, "Get behind me, Satan! You are a stumbling block to me; you do not have in mind the things of God, but the things of men." (Matthew 16:22-23) In this statement Jesus wanted Peter to know that he was being influenced by the devil.

Resurrection and Ascension

The resurrection and ascension of Jesus Christ is indisputable evidence of His divinity. Even though Jesus often spoke about His resurrection, the apostles failed to realize what He was saying. If they were unable to process the reason for His death, how could they begin to understand His resurrection from the dead? But Jesus did rise from the dead, just as He said He would. The one who had the power to forgive sins, heal the sick and raise the dead, came back to life after being tortured and crucified. This eliminated any doubt about His claim to be the Son of God. It was now time to spread the glorious news, a mission that was made possible when the apostles were empowered by the Holy Spirit. Our Savior's followers were certainly aware of the danger that they would encounter, but they were confident of Jesus' divinity, knowing that God was in their midst. There was only one life for them to pursue, that of a committed servant and messenger.

The facts surrounding Jesus' resurrection are found in the four Gospels and in the book of Acts. These writings reveal a Risen Christ who has the power over death, assuring us of our resurrection when we receive Him into our lives. Without the empty tomb, we simply have a dead martyr in the pages of history. Apart from the resurrection, Jesus is just another victim of an oppressive government that tortures and executes those who do not adhere to their political, philosophical, and religious beliefs. History is full of individuals who have given their lives for some cause. But Jesus was not a martyr, for He willingly sacrificed His life and rose from the dead to show us the way to salvation. His tomb is the only one in history that was opened by a heavenly messenger so that people might believe. Death and the grave could not hold the Son of God, and this truth was confirmed by eyewitnesses.

Historians and theologians continue to speculate and question the location of our Lord's tomb, but it is of little significance where His body was buried. What matters for the Church is that He rose from the dead. The apostles and other disciples saw our risen Savior, many of whom were persecuted or put to death for their testimony. Few people are willing to die for the truth, let alone a falsehood. During a trip to Israel, I entered the tomb in Jerusalem where many Christians believe that Jesus was laid to rest. It is in the Church of the Holy Sepulcher, which is located within the city walls. This location was outside the city during the time of Jesus, and ancient remains reveal that crucifixions occurred in this area. There is also a garden tomb that some people believe was our Savior's burial place, primarily because it may date back to the first century. The uncertainty of Jesus' burial place may be a blessing, for it should prevent believers from worshipping a place rather than the Savior. But this has not stopped people from venerating these two locations.

The Scriptures tell us that two Jewish leaders, Joseph of Arimathaea and Nicodemus, went to Pilate requesting permission to bury our Lord. Pilate agreed, and the two men wrapped the body in clean linen, using about seventy-five pounds of myrrh and aloes. This process was in accordance with the Jewish burial customs at that time. They placed Jesus' body in Joseph's personal tomb, which had been cut out of rock. While they were doing this, Mary Magdalene and another Mary were watching. (Matthew 27:57-61; Mark 15:43; John 19:38-42) Both Joseph and Nicodemus were members of the Sanhedrin, as well as secret followers of Jesus. Their concern about our Lord's body was rooted in their faith and love, for they truly believed that Jesus was the Messiah sent by God.

The Pharisees and chief priests were also concerned about Jesus' body, but it was for another reason. They anticipated that His body would be stolen by the apostles or other believers, claiming that Jesus rose from the dead. To be assured that this did not happen, they went to Pilate and asked for security measures. Pilate ordered that a guard be placed at the entrance to the tomb. The Jewish leaders added to the security by placing a seal on the entrance stone. (Matthew 27:62-66) One can only imagine Pilate's thoughts as he pondered all the concerns that revolved around Jesus. First, it was the false accusation that led to His crucifixion. Then, there were members of the Sanhedrin who wanted to bury the body. And now, Pilate is asked to place security at the tomb of a dead man. It seems that Pilate's wife was justified when she told her husband not to have anything to do with Jesus. (Matthew 27:19)

At dawn on the first day of the week, after the Sabbath was over, Mary Magdalene, Mary the mother of James, and Salome, brought spices so that they might anoint Jesus' body. The spices they brought were simply a gesture of love, offered as a farewell to the one who had changed their life. Their concern, of course, was finding a way to roll back the heavy stone at the entrance to the tomb. (Mark 16:1-3) But when they arrived, they saw that the stone had already been rolled away from the entrance. Matthew tells us that there had been a violent earthquake that was associated with the appearance of an angel, and this is when the stone was removed from the entrance of the sepulcher. Those who were assigned as security guards may have passed out before fleeing in fear. According to Matthew, the guards shook and became like dead men when they saw the angel. (Matthew 28:1-4)

The angel, who appeared in glowing white attire, announced that Jesus rose from the dead. He told the women to inform the disciples that He would see them in Galilee. Both Luke and John mention that there were two angels at the tomb. (Luke 24:4; John 20:10-12) Shortly after the women departed, Jesus appeared to them and repeated the message that the angel had given to them. Although trembling and bewildered, the women joyfully responded to Jesus, and they went to look for the apostles.

When the guards told the chief priests what had taken place, the Jewish leaders devised a plan. They gave the guards a large sum of money, telling them to spread the news that Jesus' apostles stole His body during the night. (Matthew 28:11-15) The intention was to silence any news that Jesus may have risen from the dead. After all, if Jesus had been resurrected, their positions and respect among the people would be in jeopardy. There was also a possibility that the Roman government would hold them responsible for any unrest among the Jews.

The accounts of our Savior's resurrection appearances vary, but rather than this being problematic, it is understandable. Each writer, while not diminishing the facts, gives their account of what they witnessed. Whenever there is more than one witness to an event it is natural for the details to be communicated differently. In other words, no two people will report something exactly the same way. If they do, collusion will certainly be suspected. Some people may have difficulty with variations of a biblical event, but scholars believe that such differences serve to substantiate the truth.

After the Lord's resurrection there was a period of forty days in which He appeared to His disciples. (Acts 1:3) He did not appear to them in a ghostly form, but rather as the person they knew. Jesus displayed the wounds of His torture and execution, and the apostles were invited to touch His body. He did, however, have the ability to appear and vanish at will. This occurred when He suddenly manifested himself to them while they were meeting behind locked doors. A similar situation involved two men that Jesus spent time with in the village of Emmaus. (Luke 24:30-31) But Jesus was the same person, whose words about the kingdom of God brought encouragement and hope.

The following is a chronology of our Savior's resurrection appearances as they appear in the Gospels and in the book of Acts. Because these accounts are given by different writers, the time frames are not clear:

- Mary Magdalene, Mary the mother of James, and Salome, went to the tomb at dawn on the first day of the week to apply spices to Jesus' body. When they arrived, they found the sepulcher open and the body of Jesus missing. Mary Magdalene left to tell Peter and John of the situation, while the other women remained at the tomb. (John 20:1-2; Mark 16:1-4; Luke 24:1-3)

- The women who remained at the sepulcher encountered two angels, who announced that Jesus had risen from the dead. The women were told that Jesus would see the disciples in Galilee. (Matthew 28:5-7; Mark 16:5-7; Luke 24:4-8)

- By the time Mary Magdalene returned to the tomb the other women had left. As she was weeping, she looked into the tomb and saw two angels in white, seated where Jesus' body had been. After the angels asked her why she was crying, she suddenly saw Jesus standing there. At first, she thought that He was the gardener. When she recognized Him, He immediately told her not to hold on to Him, for He had not yet returned to the Father. This statement indicates that His return to the Father was about to change His relationship with humanity. It also suggests that Jesus may have appeared before the Father prior to spending time with His disciples after He rose from the dead. Mary Magdalene went to the apostles with the news. (Mark 16:9-11; John 20:10-18)

- Jesus appeared to Mary the mother of James, and to Salome and Joanna, while they were en route to the city. He repeated His message to them, that His disciples should meet Him in Galilee. The women, along with others who were traveling with them, gave Jesus' message to the apostles. But the apostles did not believe that they had seen Jesus. (Matthew 28:8-12)

- Peter and another disciple, believed to be John, ran to the tomb and found it empty. They saw the strips of linen lying there, as well as the burial cloth that had been around Jesus' head. If the body had been stolen, the wrappings would not have been removed. The position of the wrappings also made them wonder if Jesus had risen from the dead. (Luke 24:12; John 20:3-10)

- Jesus came to Peter before He appeared to the other apostles. This is reported by both Luke and Paul, but they do not provide the circumstances. (Luke 24:34; I Corinthians 15:5)

- While on their way to the village of Emmaus, which was about seven miles from Jerusalem, two believers were approached by Jesus, one of whom was named Cleopas. At first, they did not recognize Him. Later in the day Jesus ate with them, and the men suddenly realized that the one they befriended was Jesus. Luke tells us that Jesus then disappeared from their sight. (Luke 24:13-35; Mark 16:12-13)

- Jesus appeared to the apostles when Thomas was not present. For fear of persecution, they met in a home behind locked doors. Jesus suddenly appeared in the room and showed them His hands and feet. He then said to them, "Peace be with you. As the Father has sent me, I am sending you." Jesus then breathed on them and said, "Receive the Holy Spirit." (Luke 24:36-43; John 20:19-23)

- A week later Jesus came to the apostles again, and this time Thomas was present. Thomas did not believe that the others had previously seen Jesus. He told them that he would only believe if he were able to put his finger where the nails were and place his hand into Jesus' pierced side. Jesus told Thomas to touch His wounds and to stop doubting. After doing so, Thomas said, "My Lord and my God." Jesus then said to Thomas, "Because you have seen me you have believed; blessed are those who have not seen and yet have believed." (John 20:24-29)

- The apostles went to a mountain where Jesus directed them to go. It was here that Jesus informed them that the Father had given Him authority over heaven and earth. Jesus commissioned them, saying, "Go and make disciples of all nations, baptizing them in the name of the Father and of the Son and of the Holy Spirit, and teaching them to obey everything I have commanded you, and surely I am with you always, to the very end of the age." (Matthew 28:16-20; Mark 16:15-18)

- Jesus appeared to His apostles by the Sea of Tiberius. It was early in the morning, after the apostles had a failed fishing experience the previous night. Jesus told them where to cast their net, and the results were overwhelming. Our Lord then invited them to share a breakfast of fish and bread. It was during this time that Peter was reinstated for having denied knowing Jesus after our Savior's arrest. After Peter assured Jesus of his love and commitment, Jesus commissioned him to be a shepherd of the people. (John 21:1-19)

- The apostle Paul reports that Jesus was seen by more than five hundred believers at the same time. This may have been a situation when a crowd gathered where Jesus and His apostles were reported to be. When the announcement of our Lord's resurrection spread, we can be certain that people were anxious to see Him. (I Corinthians 15:6)

- Jesus is seen by the apostle James, then by the other apostles. No other information is provided by Paul. (I Corinthians 15:7)

- In the vicinity of Bethany, the apostles witnessed Jesus' ascension. When this occurred, two angels appeared to them, saying, "Men of Galilee, why do you stand here looking into the sky? This same Jesus, who has been taken from you into heaven, will come back in the same way you have seen him go into heaven." (Mark 16:19; Luke 24:50-52; Acts 1:9-11)

- Prior to Paul accepting Jesus as his Lord and Savior, he set out on a trip to the synagogues in Damascus. He had authority from the high priest to arrest anyone, man or woman, who was a follower of Jesus. Paul's intention was to bring these individuals back to Jerusalem where they would appear before the Jewish Council. However, while he was en route, a light from heaven suddenly flashed around him. It was so intense that it caused him to lose his sight. In the midst of the light was heard the voice of Jesus questioning Paul's intentions. This was the turning point for Paul and the beginning of a life that was given to preaching the Gospel. (Acts 9:1-31)

Jesus did not appear to the religious leaders or Roman officials who would again seek His arrest and execution, believing that they were somehow tricked the first time. It was God's will that He would only appear to believers, who would take His message to the world. Without an attitude of repentance and faith the hearts of people do not change, which was the case with the religious authorities.

DOCTRINE OF THE TRINITY

The early Church debated the nature of God, which included the relationship between Jesus and God the Father. There was also dialogue that focused upon whether the *Trinity* is a different manifestation of one Divine Person, or if the nature of God comprises three distinct personalities within one Deity. Questions relating to the nature of God officially began with the Council of Nicaea, which took place in A.D. 325. This dialogue continued through the second Council at Constantinople in A.D. 381. It is this council that confirmed the Deity of the Holy Spirit, referring to the Spirit as "the Lord and Giver of life, who proceeds from the Father, who is to be worshipped and glorified with the Father and Son, and who spoke through the prophets." At the third Synod of Toledo in A.D. 589, it was asserted that the Holy Spirit proceeds from both the Father and Son. This was the primary cause for the division between the Western and Eastern Churches.

The word *Trinity* is not found in the Bible, but the Hebrew Scriptures do provide insight into this mystery. For example, in the Genesis account of the creation story we find God saying, "Let *us* make man in *our image*, in *our likeness*." (Genesis 1:26) Another passage that uses the plural for God is given by the prophet Isaiah. It reads, "Then I heard the voice of the Lord saying, 'Whom shall I send? And who will go for *us*?'" (Isaiah 6:8) Scholars offer other scripture that they believe indicate a plurality within God, but I find them questionable.

The concept of the *Trinity* was first employed in the second century by Tertullian, who was a Roman author and early Church father (A.D. 160-230). He emphasized that this doctrine is clearly revealed in the New Testament. The apostle Paul wrote the Ephesians that there is "one Lord, one faith, one baptism, one God and Father of all, who is over all and through all and in all." (Ephesians 4:5-6; Hebrews 1:8) Two passages revealing a Triune God are Matthew 28:19, which is our Savior's commission to the apostles, and a benediction given by Paul that is found in II Corinthians 13:14. A graphic picture of the *Trinity* is revealed with the baptism of Jesus, in which we are simultaneously aware of the three Persons of the Godhead. As Jesus was being baptized by John in the Jordan River, the Spirit of God descended upon Him like a dove. At the same time, the Father's voice is heard acknowledging Jesus as His Son. (Matthew 3:13-17)

After extensive study, prayer and dialogue, the Church has concluded that within the Godhead there are three eternal and co-equal Persons who are the same in substance, yet different in subsistence. While they have distinct personalities and functions, all three Persons share the same essence, have always existed, act in unity, and possess the same will for creation and humanity. Because the mystery of the *Trinity* is beyond our comprehension, we accept this doctrine in faith, based upon the Scriptures and the prayers of the early Church. Those who say more on this matter are merely voicing speculation. There may be a time when the Lord provides increased understanding, but it will not be in this life.

RECEIVING THE HOLY SPIRIT

From the Hebrew Bible we know that God's Spirit acted upon the lives of people in different ways, providing individuals with understanding, knowledge, power and guidance. Some biblical figures were said to have internalized the Holy Spirit, meaning that the Spirit lived within them. Such was the case with Joseph, of whom Pharaoh said, "Can we find anyone like this man, one *in whom* is the Spirit of God?" (Genesis 41:38) Another example of the indwelling Spirit is Joshua. The Lord said to Moses, "Take Joshua, son of Nun, a man *in whom* is the Spirit, and lay your hand on him." (Numbers 27:18) After King David committed adultery with Bathsheba and plotted the death of her husband Uriah, the prophet Nathan confronted him with his sins. In his guilt and sorrow, David cried out to God, "Do not cast me from your presence or take your Holy Spirit from me." (Psalm 51:11)

We cannot be certain from these Old Testament passages if the Holy Spirit temporarily empowered these individuals or actually resided within them. We do know, however, that the movement of the Spirit is found throughout biblical history. Although we may question the extent of the Holy Spirit's involvement with humanity, the Spirit's presence is certain. The prophet Ezekiel provides clear instances when God's Spirit was moving upon the people. In fact, it was Ezekiel and the prophet Joel who spoke about a future time when God's Spirit would reside within the hearts of people. Concerning Israel, God spoke through Ezekiel, saying, "I will give you a new heart and put a new spirit in you. I will put my Spirit in you and move you to follow my decrees and be careful to keep my laws." (Ezekiel 36:26-27) But it was Joel who prophesied about a future outpouring of the Holy Spirit upon all people, a truth that is realized through Jesus Christ. Joel wrote, "And it shall come to pass that I will pour out my Spirit upon all people. Your sons and daughters will prophesy, your old men will dream dreams, your young men will see visions. Even on my servants, both men and women, I will pour out my Spirit in those days." (Joel 2:28-29)

John the Baptist preached that the followers of Jesus would be baptized with the purifying fire of the Holy Spirit. (Matthew 3:11) It was on Pentecost that the apostles received the power of the Holy Spirit. This is why Jesus told them to stay in Jerusalem until they were clothed with power from on high. (Luke 24:49) Our Savior made it clear that His followers needed the power and gifts that only the Spirit can provide. It is this power that convicts us of our sins, leads us to repentance, and cleanses the inner person. (John 3:5; Hebrews 9:14)

Jesus taught that the Holy Spirit gives life, emphasizing that the flesh counts for nothing. (John 6:63) He referred to the Holy Spirit as the Comforter, Counselor, and the Spirit of Truth, who dwells within believers, teaching them all things and empowering them for service. (John 14:15-17; 16:7-11) Jesus also said, "When the Counselor comes, whom I will send to you from the Father, the Spirit of truth who goes out from the Father, he will testify about me. And you also must testify, for you have been with me from the beginning." (John 15:26-27) In this statement Jesus was telling His disciples that the Holy Spirit would assure them of His divinity. As the apostles faced the challenges of their mission, which included intense persecution, they needed the continuous strength of the Holy Spirit.

All gifts are received through God's Spirit, including the faith that we experience and proclaim. To receive the Holy Spirit is to be free of legalism and works righteousness, both of which are rooted in sin. (II Corinthians 3:6) The Spirit moves us from spiritual death to life, enabling us to love all people, including our enemies. Through the baptism of the Holy Spirit we become new people who, although not perfect, seek to be at peace with everyone. Our desires change, with self-centeredness and pride being replaced with love for God and one another. Paul wrote his friend and co-worker Titus that we are not saved because of the righteous things that we do. Instead, it is through God's mercy and the cleansing power of the Holy Spirit. (Titus 3:4-7) Paul told the believers in Corinth that our bodies are the temple of the Holy Spirit; therefore, we must guard against all unrighteousness. (I Corinthians 3:16-17)

Jesus assured His disciples that God would supply them with the necessary gifts to preach the Gospel. He told them not to worry about defending themselves or what they should say when confronted with resistance, for the Holy Spirit would provide the courage and words. (Luke 12:11-12) Just as Jesus was instructed by the Father, they would be led by the Spirit in all things. All that was needed on their part was faith and communicating the love of Christ in all situations. (Romans 5:5; Colossians 1:7-8) Paul wrote Timothy that God did not give us a spirit of timidity, but one of power, love and self-discipline. (II Timothy 1:7) We must remember this when undertaking difficult tasks.

The gifts of the Holy Spirit are too numerous to mention in this writing, but it is important that we note particular ones. Paul points out that the Spirit has an essential part in our prayer life. In his epistle to the Romans, he said, "We do not know what we ought to pray for, but the Spirit himself intercedes for us with groans that words cannot express." (Romans 8:26) This means that the Holy Spirit takes our inexpressible feelings and stilted words, lifting them up to the Father in the form of prayer. This includes the heavy burdens that we carry for others. Sometimes we are at a loss for words or simply do not know what is best for other people, but the Spirit knows the hearts of all people and intercedes for us. In his letter to the Ephesians, Paul offers the following insights into the gifts of the Holy Spirit:

> Now to each one the manifestation of the Spirit is given for the common good. To one there is given through the Spirit the message of wisdom, to another the message of knowledge by means of the same Spirit,

to another the gifts of healing by that one Spirit, to another miraculous powers, to another prophecy, to another distinguishing between spirits, to another speaking in different kinds of tongues. All these are the work of one and the same Spirit, and he gives them to each one, just as he determines. (I Corinthians 12:7-11)

Paul emphasizes that we must live as children of light, internalizing and sharing the fruit of the Spirit. As we walk in the Spirit, we will have the desire and ability to be at peace with one another. He said, "Make every effort to keep the unity of the Spirit through the bond of peace. There is one body and one Spirit. Be completely humble and gentle, be patient, bearing with one another in love." (Ephesians 4:3-6) In another letter, Paul informed his readers that the gifts of the Spirit include: love, joy, peace, kindness, goodness, and self-control. (Galatians 5:22-23)

The Scriptures speak about blasphemy against the Holy Spirit, stating that it is an unpardonable sin. This has caused considerable discussion and debate over the years, particularly among theologians. If Jesus teaches that all sins can be forgiven, which even includes the taking of another person's life, then this passage is problematic. I cannot resolve this issue, but I can offer some food for thought. First, is it possible that Old Testament thought based upon the law is manifested in this statement? In other words, this may have been a belief before the age of grace that has come through Jesus Christ. The penalties given under Mosaic Law were quite harsh, and this statement may reflect the early legal code of the Jews.

Another explanation relates to the sin of attributing to Satan the miracles that Jesus performed through the Holy Spirit. (Matthew 12:22-32) But this would necessitate a continuous and willful rejection of realized truth as it relates to Christ and the Holy Spirit. It seems plausible that intentional and continuous sin is a key here. Paul claims to have been the worst of sinners, but when Paul discovered the truth, he repented of his sins and asked Jesus Christ into his life, receiving God's complete forgiveness and the gifts of the Spirit. It is willful and continuous evil that blocks the work of the Holy Spirit. This is the situation that speaks to our point in question.

The Holy Spirit also has a part in our resurrection. Jesus rose from the dead through the power of the Holy Spirit. Peter wrote, "Christ was put to death in the body but made alive through the Spirit." (I Peter 3:18) According to Paul, this same Spirit will raise us. He said, "If the Spirit of him who raised Jesus from the dead is living in you, he who raised Christ from the dead will also give life to your mortal bodies through his Spirit, who lives in you." (Romans 8:11) These are words of joy and hope for everyone who lives in faith. The promises that begin in the present will be fully realized through the indwelling presence of the Holy Spirit.

THE END TIMES

Eschatology is the branch of theology that examines the events relating to the end of this age and the ushering in of God's eternal kingdom. According to the Scriptures, these events will take place at the Second Advent of Jesus Christ. The kingdom of God is two-fold, for it is within us and yet to be fulfilled when Jesus returns. At our Savior's ascension, the angels informed the apostles that Jesus would return in the same manner as He left. Jesus often spoke about His return, a truth that the apostles reveal in their writings. Actually, it was believed that Jesus would return during the lifetime of the apostles. When it became apparent that this was not going to occur, the apostles recorded the life and ministry of Jesus for future generations, emphasizing His divinity and offer of forgiveness and salvation.

For years, people have been predicting when Jesus will return. Some individuals and groups have even given specific dates. Other people view world events, and they try to fit them into the book of Revelation. By doing this, they place the Second Coming of Christ into a particular time frame. But those who are making eschatological predictions are disregarding the Scriptures and our Savior's words. Jesus clearly states that no one knows the day or hour of His return, not Him or the angels in heaven. It is the Father's decision in accordance with His providence and will. In fact, since we do not know the day or hour of Jesus' return, we must make every effort to be prepared. This means living a committed life that is rooted in faith and love. (Mark 13:32-37) The parable of the *Ten Virgins* is a graphic picture of how we must keep our lamps of faith burning. If you are familiar with the parable, you know that five of the ten virgins allowed their lamps to run out of oil, and they were not prepared for the appearance of the bridegroom. They never imagined that the bridegroom would come at midnight. (Matthew 25:1-13; Luke 12:35-40) We do not know when Jesus will return; therefore, we must be vigilant by keeping our lamps of faith burning.

People questioned the apostles about their claim that Jesus would return. After all, years had gone by, and there was no indication of another appearance by our Savior. Peter spoke to this issue when he wrote, "They will say, where is this coming that he promised? Ever since our fathers died, everything goes on as it has since the beginning of creation." (II Peter 3:3-4) Peter told fellow Christians that "with the Lord a day is like a thousand years and a thousand years are like a day. The Lord is not slow about his promises, as some understand slowness. He is patient toward us, not wanting anyone to perish, but everyone to come to repentance." (II Peter 3:8-9) Peter wanted inquisitors to know that God's patience means salvation for people who otherwise would not have received Jesus Christ.

Jesus stresses that His return will be sudden and when least expected. He compared it to a flash of lightning across the sky. Paul says that Jesus' return will be like a thief in the night. (I Thessalonians 5:1-3) When Jesus returns life will be status quo, with people going about their routines and business. His unexpected return will not allow time for repentance and a change of heart; therefore, everyone's destiny will be sealed. (Luke 17:20-37) Jesus has given us graphic imagery and a strong warning about the events relating to his Second Coming. He said that His appearance will be preceded by cosmic signs. Luke shares our Lord's words:

> There will be signs in the sun, moon and stars.
> On earth, nations will be in anguish and perplexity
> at the roaring and tossing of the sea. Men will faint

from terror, apprehension of what is coming on the world, for the heavenly bodies will be shaken. At that time, they will see the Son of Man coming in a cloud with power and great glory. When these things begin to take place, stand up and lift up your heads, because your redemption is drawing near. (Luke 21:25-28)

In the parable of the *Fishing Net*, Jesus said that angels will come down from heaven and separate the wicked from the righteous. (Matthew 13:47-50) The saints who are alive when Jesus appears will be taken up to meet their Savior in the air. Jesus will be accompanied by those who have died in faith and awaiting His glorious appearance. The unrepentant will be left for judgment and thrown into the fiery furnace, where there will be weeping and gnashing of teeth. This language was meant to communicate unrelenting pain and hopelessness. (Matthew 13:49-50)

God's eternal kingdom will be realized after the destruction of this planet. This truth is given to us in both the Hebrew Scriptures and the New Testament. The prophets Isaiah and Malachi wrote about the earth's destruction and how God will create a new heaven and earth. (Isaiah 66:22; Malachi 4) Peter emphasized this cosmic event, saying, "The day of the Lord will come like a thief. The heavens will disappear with a roar; the elements will be destroyed by fire, and the earth and everything in it will be laid bare." (II Peter 3:10) In a vision, the apostle John saw "a new heaven and earth, for the first heaven and earth had passed away, and there was no longer any sea."

John also saw a new Jerusalem coming down out of heaven. These words clearly reveal that there will be a new creation for God's people. (Revelation 21:1-8)

Some Christians in Thessalonica were concerned about those who had died in Christ, believing that they may not have the joy of participating in the Second Advent of Jesus. It seems that there was confusion regarding those who died as believers. In response to these questions, Paul said:

> Brothers, we do not want you to be ignorant about those who fall asleep, or to grieve like the rest of men, who have no hope. We believe that Jesus died and rose again and so we believe that God will bring with Jesus those who have fallen asleep in him. According to the Lord's own word, we tell you that we who are still alive, who are left till the coming of the Lord, will certainly not precede those who have fallen asleep. For the Lord himself will come down from heaven, with a loud command, with the voice of the archangel and with the trumpet call of God, and the dead in Christ will rise first. After that, we who are still alive will be caught up together with them in the clouds to meet the Lord in the air. And so, we will be with the Lord forever. Therefore encourage each other with these words. (I Thessalonians 4:13-18)

When Christians die their spirits ascend to God's realm, which the Scriptures refer to as *heaven* or *Paradise*. They remain in this state of peace and rest awaiting the Second

Advent of Christ. The parable of *Lazarus and the Rich Man* provides some insight into this place of perfection, where we experience the presence of God. (Luke 16:19-31) Although we are not given the details of this intermediate state, the parable suggests that we will be conscious of our heavenly bliss. Unrepentant sinners will also be aware of their separation from the Lord.

FINAL JUDGMENT

The traditional belief is that there will be one general judgment. According to the Scriptures, the authority to judge the world has been given to Jesus by God the Father. It is also clear that everyone will stand before Christ to give an account of their lives. We may not know the specifics relating to God's judgment, but it will occur when Jesus returns at the end of this age. It will be a time of great joy for the faithful and one of anguish for the unrepentant. The apostle John was given a vision in which he saw the judgment of the unsaved:

> Then I saw a great white throne and him who was seated on it. Earth and sky fled from his presence, and there was no place for them. And I saw the dead, great and small, standing before the throne, and books were opened. Another book was opened, which is the Book of Life. The dead were judged according to what they had done as recorded in the book. The sea gave up the dead that were in it, and death and Hades gave up the dead that were in them, and each person was judged according to what he had done. Then death

and Hades were thrown into the lake of fire. The lake of fire is the second death. If anyone's name was not found in the Book of Life, he was thrown into the lake of fire. (Revelation 20:11-15)

According to John's vision, those who are not found in the Book of Life will be eternally separated from the Lord's presence. The judgment of the unsaved will include the fallen angels who abandoned their positions of authority. They have been kept in darkness, bound with everlasting chains for judgment. (Jude 6) Peter wrote, "For God did not spare angels when they sinned, but sent them to hell, putting them in gloomy dungeons to be held for judgment." (II Peter 2:4; I Corinthians 6:3) These words may be interpreted as being separated from God while awaiting judgment. The angels who followed Satan, bringing evil into the world, will eternally be held accountable for their pride and sinful actions.

Believers will also stand before the throne of Jesus Christ, but it will not be a judgment that relates to sin. The sins of the faithful have been atoned for and forgotten by God. (II Corinthians 5:10; Hebrews 10:17) Although the saved have repented of their sins and live in the promises of Jesus, it is necessary that their lives be examined at the time of judgment. (Matthew 12:36; Romans 14:10; Ephesians 6:8; I Corinthians 3:11-15) Before entering God's eternal kingdom we will be given an overview of our lives, which will show us both the positive and negative influences that we have had upon others.

THE CHURCH

Should anyone attempt to critique the contemporary Church, with all of its denominations and splinter groups? To traverse this ground will certainly bring responses from those who wish to protect their turf. But if governments and other institutions are not exempt from scrutiny, why should the Church be an exception? After all, the Scriptures tell us that we must continuously examine ourselves in light of our Savior's teachings. We are aware of the sins that have made their way into holy places and the need to purge the Church of evil. If the type of sins that are found in the Church were to exist in other institutions, we can be certain that they would be confronted.

But sin is not the only issue that plagues Christian congregations and dampens the human spirit. There are many areas that divide people, such as: the understanding of biblical inspiration and inerrancy, the interpretation of certain biblical passages, the sacraments, eschatology, traditions, and sexual beliefs. There are also differences in the way people worship. Some churches are very liturgical, while others openly express their joy during worship. These and other differences have eroded the unity that God commands. Rather than being united in the spirit of love and faith, the Church has become divided. The Scriptures repeatedly call for the unity that makes us strong witnesses for Christ, but what we find is separation. Rather than focusing upon the salvation that we share in Christ, our differences have created pride and suspicion.

The institutional Church has both enlightened me and brought discouragement and frustration. At times, it has even caused me to lose the joy that Jesus promises believers. The teachings of our Savior, when properly communicated, are a source of excitement and hope. But the endless issues and power struggles in some churches are dispiriting. How can people who repeatedly hear the teachings of Jesus fail to internalize His lessons on love and forgiveness? If we claim to walk in the Spirit, then the gifts of the Spirit should be manifested in our lives. Everyone is at a different place in their spiritual journey, but all Christians should be living the essentials of their faith. Are Christian ministries failing people, or are there other factors involved? What is the responsibility of the Church, as opposed to that of individuals when it comes to spiritual development?

Clergy must encourage parishioners to develop a spiritual life beyond the church building. Those who look only to church ministry for their spiritual needs will never grow in faith and understanding. How can anyone believe that an hour or two a week will meet their deepest needs? On the other hand, are pastors and other spiritual leaders providing the Christian education that challenges people and strengthens their faith? Most congregations have a written statement that defines their beliefs and mission, but few people know the content of these writings. Once these statements are completed, the dust of complacency keeps them hidden from view. When the promises relating to spiritual growth and community outreach are not kept, congregations lose their way.

Those in leadership positions are often more concerned about buildings and bank accounts than with Christian education and community work. This may sound like a harsh judgment, but after thirty-five years in the ministry I have often found this to be true. Every congregation must focus upon their true mission—that of preaching the Gospel, Christian education, and community outreach. This means that prayer and adjustments must be a continuing part of ministry. It is doubtful that many congregations gather together to seek the Lord's guidance in these areas.

How would Jesus define His Church and mission? Although many generations have passed since Jesus walked this earth, our Lord's intentions for His Church have not changed. But some faith groups have taken a different path, moving away from our Savior's teachings and mission. Secularism, rigid structures, and poor leadership, are just a few reasons why the Church has lost its way. In Revelation we hear Jesus' strong statements to seven congregations that lost sight of their calling. He warned them about false teachings, the influences of sin, losing their focus, and becoming lukewarm. It is interesting that these same problems exist today. (Revelation 2-3)

The Church experienced its birth on Pentecost, when the Holy Spirit anointed the apostles, giving them the gifts and power to proclaim the Gospel to people from different regions. Pentecost, which was a celebration that related to the harvest, brought large crowds to Jerusalem, and the apostles were led by God to preach the message of salvation to those entering the city. The travelers were perplexed because the apostles were able to speak in their native languages. Although some Christians today understand this gift to be a spiritual communication that only certain individuals can interpret, the apostles were speaking in known languages of their day. Saint Luke recorded what took place:

When the day of Pentecost came, they were all together in one place. Suddenly, a sound like the blowing of a violent wind came from heaven and filled the whole house where they were sitting. They saw what seemed to be tongues of fire that separated and came to rest on each of them. All of them were filled with the Holy Spirit and began speaking in other tongues as the Spirit enabled them. Now there were staying in Jerusalem God-fearing Jews from every nation under heaven. When they heard this sound, a crowd came together in bewilderment, because each one heard them speaking in his own language. (Acts 2:1-6)

Before His ascension, Jesus promised His apostles that He would send the Holy Spirit, who would give them power to proclaim the Gospel and be His witnesses. On Pentecost this work began, with three thousand people becoming baptized believers. (Acts 2:14-41) What followed was an evangelistic mission that led to persecution and martyrdom. Being filled with the Holy Spirit and doing God's will does not remove us from trials and persecution. According to tradition, eleven of the twelve apostles were martyred for their faith and mission work. Paul, who was not one of the original twelve apostles, was also martyred for preaching the Gospel. He was beheaded by the Roman government during the reign of Nero.

After Pentecost, it was customary for the apostles to meet together for prayer, mutual encouragement, and some manner of worship. Because they feared persecution and arrest, they met in private homes. The early Christians found it necessary to gather together, but they never viewed the Church in terms of a building. The apostles were commissioned by Jesus to continue His work, but our Savior never intended His Church to be comprised of cathedrals and separate denominations. The early Church was understood to be individuals of faith who were empowered by the Holy Spirit to be active participants in serving God. Like their Master, the focus was upon being a servant. Just as Jesus was always on the move, His followers did the same, knowing the significance of time and opportunities. Rather than building projects and ministry that only related to them, it was about reaching everyone for whom Jesus sacrificially gave His life. Instead of filling up church pews, they saw themselves as the salt of the earth. To stay in the salt shaker was not doing the Lord's work. What a lesson for Christians today, whose lives revolve around particular faith communities and church structures.

While gathering places are necessary, our building project does not involve mortar, steel and brick. It is living the humble life of a servant and sharing God's love wherever we happen to be. Buildings have a purpose, but when they replace the true Church, we lose our witness for Jesus Christ. God wants living stones to build His kingdom, those who will follow in the footsteps of Jesus. To understand successful ministry in terms of buildings, budgets and Sunday morning attendance, is a misconception of the Church. Millions of dollars have been spent on church buildings and complexes, while the poor continue to struggle with basic needs. Is this the Church that Jesus intended?

Jesus spoke about the nature of His Church in a response to the apostle Peter. When Peter manifested his faith in Jesus as the Son of God, our Savior said to him, "You are Peter, and upon this rock I will build my Church, and the gates of Hades will not overcome it." (Matthew 16:18) Peter's name was Simon, but Jesus changed his surname to Peter, which in Greek is translated *Rock*. Our Lord did this because of Simon's inner strength and commitment. This is not suggesting that Peter initially had strong faith, but our Lord knew that Peter had the character that would develop into a strong witness. Peter was ultimately martyred for his faith, asking that he be crucified upside down because he did not feel worthy of dying in the same manner as his Savior. Rather than cathedrals, the Church of Jesus Christ lies within the hearts of those who offer themselves up as living sacrifices to the Lord.

Our Lord's response has resulted with some Christians believing that the Church has been built upon the apostle Peter. This is stating that the Church of Jesus Christ is built upon a man. Is this what Jesus meant, or should we understand it differently? Since our salvation is rooted in our faith, one must conclude that Jesus was alluding to Peter's unwavering trust in Him as Lord and Savior. Every New Testament writer emphasizes that we are saved by God's grace and our personal faith in Jesus Christ. Paul stresses this truth throughout his writings. The Church is comprised of people from every nation and culture who have surrendered their lives to Jesus, trusting in His promises and power. Regardless of trials and times of discouragement, their faith is steadfast.

GOSPEL OF LOVE AND FORGIVENESS

The central message of Christianity is God's love for humanity and His offer of forgiveness and reconciliation through Jesus Christ. The good news of salvation excludes no one, for Jesus offered up His life for every sinner. Although elementary, this central truth often gets lost amid legalism, worldliness, and the issues that plague congregations. It is God's love that sent Jesus to live among us, experiencing the trials that led to His agonizing death on the cross. While there are important lessons to be learned from the Hebrew Scriptures, which we refer to as the Old Testament, we now live in the age of grace. This means that the teachings of Jesus and the apostles must take precedence in our ministries. It is interesting that some pastors spend more time preaching from Old Testament law than they do from the Gospels and other New Testament writings.

God gave the law to Israel as a precursor to the coming of Jesus, with His sacrifice replacing the sacrifices of the Levitical system. While the laws of the Old Testament were divinely given and had their purpose, they have been fulfilled in Jesus Christ. In his epistle to the Galatians, Paul said, "we who are Jews by birth and not Gentile sinners, know that a man is not justified by observing the law, but by faith in Jesus Christ. So, we too, have put our faith in Jesus Christ that we may be justified by faith in Christ and not by observing the law, because by observing the law no one will be justified." (Galatians 2:15-16)

The law was given to magnify sin and to show Israel how far they were from God. It was designed to sear the conscience and bring about repentance, accountability, and spiritual transformation. As such, it was intended to lead people to a faith relationship with God. But the Jews, particularly the religious leaders, used their outer obedience as a vehicle for pride. They failed to realize that true obedience is a matter of the heart, which the law alone cannot change. It is only through the love of Christ that our hearts change, enabling us to obey the law in the spirit of love. When Jesus is our Savior, we have both the desire and power to love God and one another.

Apart from the love and sacrifice of Jesus Christ, there is no justification or righteousness before God. It was the Father's love that sent His Son into our lives, and now it is through the Son that we are forgiven and reconciled to the Father. The parable of the *Prodigal Son* reveals the Father's infinite and unconditional love. Even when we become filled with pride and rebellion, the Father is willing to forgive and allow us to return home where His grace abides. (Luke 15:11-32) Paul reminds us that the death of Jesus was for sinners of every generation. (Romans 5:6-9) The apostle John, whose writings emphasize the divinity and love of Jesus, wrote:

> In all things God works for the good of those who love him, who have been called according to his purpose. If God is for us, who can be against us? He who did not spare his own Son, but gave him up for us all—how will he not also, along with him, graciously give us all things? For I am convinced that neither death nor life, neither angels nor demons, neither the present nor the future, nor any powers, neither height

nor depth, nor anything else in all creation, will be able to separate us from the love of God that is in Christ Jesus our Lord. (Romans 8:28-39)

We are not transformed and saved through Old Testament law, but rather by the grace of God that flows through His Son. As a pastor I have always told new Christians to feed upon the teachings of Jesus and the apostles, for this is where salvation and God's grace is found. Again, this is not to imply that the Hebrew Bible should be cast aside. As God's inspired Word, it has a sacred place in the Church. But New Testament writings must take precedence if we are to grow in love and understanding. During my years of theological education and ministry, I have certainly found value in Old Testament writings. However, it is the words of Jesus that have pierced my heart and brought me into a saving relationship with God. Jesus is our reason for being and the only hope that we have, and His words must be at the center of our ministries and life. He is the revelation of God's love to a lost and dying world, and to lose His message is to lose our mission in life.

There was a certain time when many of Jesus' followers deserted Him. This was after He spoke about His death and told the people that they must eat His flesh and drink His blood. Some people had difficulty understanding the meaning of His figurative language. Others were leaving Jesus because they wanted Him to be a political leader who would confront the Roman government. On one occasion Jesus asked His apostles if they also were going to leave Him. In response, Peter answered, "Lord, to whom shall we go? You have the words of eternal life. We believe and know that you are the Holy One of God." (John 6:60-69)

Everyone knows individuals who have low self-esteem and live with a defeatist attitude. These feelings may lead to self-destructive and life-threatening acts. Having served in both law enforcement and as a state prison chaplain, I have interacted with many people who have difficulty loving themselves. These feelings may result from family of origin issues, a mental or physical handicap, a sense of failure, or the lack of meaningful relationships. But whatever the reason, they believe that they are worthless. Such people need to know that God equally loves all of His children, regardless where they are in life. Rather than the law, it is through the teachings of the New Testament that these hurting individuals are healed.

Mark informs us about a teacher of the law who asked Jesus which of God's commandments is the most important. Jesus answered, "Love the Lord your God with all your heart and with all your soul and with all your mind and with all your strength. The second is this: Love your neighbor as yourself. There is no commandment greater than these." (Mark 12:28-31) These two commandments are inseparable, for we cannot love others if the love of God is not in us. Also, how can we claim to love the Lord, if we fail to love those for whom Jesus died? Sometimes we forget that loving and forgiving others is a salvation issue. Jesus clearly taught that our forgiveness is based upon us loving and forgiving others from the heart.

Love and forgiveness also relate to those whom we perceive to be our enemies. I heard a preacher say that love is the unconquerable weapon, and I have found this to be true.

While there are always exceptions, it is difficult to hate someone who loves you and shows it in concrete ways. A person may not openly respond to our acts of love, but it is doubtful that they will speak out against us. When we think about giving up on others, we should remember that God never gives up on us. We must realize that, although God hates sin, He loves the person. This is why Jesus gave His life for every sinner. Our Savior told His disciples that they were to love their enemies and pray for those who mistreated them. To accentuate this, He said:

> If you love those who love you, what credit is that to you? Even sinners love those who love them. And if you do good to those who are good to you, what credit is that to you? Even sinners do that. And if you lend to those from whom you expect payment, what credit is that to you? Even sinners lend to sinners, expecting to be repaid in full. But love your enemies, do good to them, and lend to them without expecting to get anything back. Then your reward will be great, and you will be sons of the Most High, because he is kind to the ungrateful and wicked. Be merciful, just as your Father is merciful. (Luke 6:32-36)

It is not only important that we pray for our enemies, but we must also pray about our negative feelings toward them. We may even be led to put our prayers into concrete forms of love. It is easy to say that we love someone who has offended us, but words often ring shallow without some manner of action.

Praying about conflictive relationships always brings positive results, even if it is only our heart and attitude that changes. Paul told Christians that they were to live in peace with everyone, stating that revenge belongs to God alone. To the church in Rome, he wrote:

> Do not repay anyone evil for evil. Be careful to do what is right in the eyes of everybody. If it is possible, as far as it depends on you, live at peace with everyone. Do not take revenge my friends, but leave room for God's wrath. For it is written: "It is mine to avenge; I will repay," says the Lord. On the contrary: If your enemy is hungry, feed him; if he is thirsty, give him something to drink. In doing this, you will heap burning coals on his head. Do not be overcome by evil, but overcome evil with good. (Romans 12:17-21)

Paul's focus upon love and being a servant of God are repetitious themes in his writings. He said, "Let no debt remain outstanding, except the continuing debt to love one another, for he who loves his fellow man has fulfilled the law." (Romans 13:8) He told believers that they should carry each other's burdens and honor others above themselves. (Romans 12:10; Galatians 6:2) In his letter to the church in Corinth he wrote that love is the greatest gift, even more valuable and meaningful than faith and hope. He stressed how our life and accomplishments are empty without the love of Christ in our hearts. He called love the most excellent way, saying:

> If I speak in the tongues of men and of angels, but have not love, I am only a resounding gong or a clanging cymbal. If I have the gift of prophecy, and can fathom all mysteries and all knowledge, and if I have a faith that can move mountains, but have not love, I am nothing. If I give all I possess to the poor and surrender my body to the flames, but have not love, I gain nothing. Love is patient, love is kind. It does not envy, it does not boast, it is not proud. It is not rude, it is not self-seeking, it is not easily angered, it keeps no record of wrongs. Love does not delight in evil but rejoices with the truth. It always protects, always trusts, always hopes, always perseveres. Love never fails. And now these three remain: faith, hope, and love. But the greatest of these is love. (I Corinthians 13:1-13)

Humility is essential for loving God and one another, a truth that Paul focused upon in his epistle to the Philippians. He told them that they must never do anything out of vain conceit, but rather to practice humility in all situations. He said that one's attitude should be the same as that of Jesus who, although the Son of God, did not place Himself above the humanity that He created. Instead, He took upon Himself the nature of a humble servant and carried the weight of humanity's sins, even giving His life for us. (Philippians 2:1-11) Jesus taught His disciples that the greatest gift is living the life of a humble servant, who shows mercy to all people. He told them that God causes the sun to rise on the evil and the good, and He sends rain on the righteous and unrighteous. (Matthew 5:43-48) When the apostles were debating which of them was the greatest, Jesus quickly responded by saying, "If anyone wants to be first, he must be the very last and the servant of all." (Mark 9:35) This was the life that Jesus lived on earth, and He commands that His followers do the same. When our Savior washed the feet of His apostles, He was giving them a graphic example of being a servant. After doing this, He said to them:

> You call me Teacher and Lord, and rightly so, for that is what I am. Now that I, your Lord and Teacher, have washed your feet, you also should wash one another's feet. I have set you an example that you should do as I have done for you. I tell you the truth, no servant is greater than his master, nor is a messenger greater than the one who sent him. Now that you know these things, you will be blessed if you do them. (John 13:12-17)

Our Savior's parable of *The Good Samaritan* is an example of what it means to be a servant. The Jews did not associate with the Samaritans, believing that they were inferior. Because of mixed marriages, primarily with Assyrians, they were only part Jewish. But it was a Samaritan who stopped and rendered assistance to a Jew who was assaulted and robbed. While a Jewish priest and a Levite temple worker made a detour around the bleeding man, the one considered to be an outcast did not hesitate to stop. The Samaritan did everything he could to help restore the man's health. He bandaged his wounds, put him on his own donkey, and took him to an inn for additional care. He even paid the innkeeper for all the expenses. (Luke 10:25-37) Like the Samaritan in our story, true servants of God cross all religious, cultural, and racial lines. They respond to the needs of others regardless of the circumstances. According to the apostle John, these are the individuals who have passed from death to life. (I John 3:14-15)

With the anticipation of His departure, Jesus knew that His apostles needed God's love in their hearts. While speaking to them about His imminent betrayal and death, He said, "A new command I give you: Love one another. As I have loved you, so you must love one another. By this all men will know that you are my disciples, if you love one another." (John 13:34-35) Jesus knew that this was a new command for His apostles, for the Jews resisted loving those who were outside of their culture and faith system. Our Lord's apostles could not be witnesses of God's love unless they were able to love all people, and this included their enemies.

BIBLICAL INSPIRATION AND INERRANCY

Although the Church believes in the inspiration of the Bible, there are different understandings of this doctrine. Some Christians adhere to biblical inerrancy, which essentially states that the Bible is without error in all matters relating to our lives. This, of course, poses many questions. Others take a more liberal view of the Scriptures and God's involvement with the writers. The apostle Paul wrote that "all Scripture is God-breathed and is useful for teaching, rebuking, correcting, and training in righteousness, so that the man of God may be thoroughly equipped for every good work." (II Timothy 3:16-17)

Paul believed that both the Hebrew Bible and the New Testament are inspired by God. His teachings tell us that the Scriptures are the result of God's direct involvement with the writers. The extent of the Lord's involvement and how the Scriptures apply to us today continues to be questioned by Christians.

God directed the prophets to communicate His truths and commands to the people. Their words often related to warnings, as well as words of hope. Examples of this are found with Moses and Jeremiah. (Exodus 17:14; Jeremiah 30:2) These scriptures seem to indicate that the Lord actually dictated what He wanted written. Can we use these examples throughout the Scriptures, or were the writers free to use their own style and words to convey God's messages? These questions persist, and it is doubtful that they will be resolved. What matters most is that the Bible provides inspired words that lead to salvation and righteous living.

Paul believed that the Holy Spirit spoke directly to the prophets. In a letter to the Galatians, he quoted an Old Testament scripture that prophetically points to Jesus Christ. In this reference Paul was specific about the wording and interpretation, indicating his belief that God was in every word. (Galatians 3:16; Acts 28:25-27) Paul even acknowledged that he and his fellow apostles wrote through the inspiration of the Holy Spirit. To the Corinthians, he said, "This is what we speak, not in words taught us by human wisdom but in words taught by the Spirit, expressing spiritual truths in spiritual words." (I Corinthians 2:13)

Peter believed that the prophets were inspired writers who not only communicated God's messages concerning the lives of the Jews, but that they also echoed prophetic words relating to the grace that would be realized in Jesus Christ. Peter stated that the prophets searched the Scriptures in an attempt to know the circumstances regarding the future Messiah, who would change the hearts and lives of future generations. To the Christians in Asia Minor, he wrote:

> Concerning this salvation, the prophets, who spoke of the grace that was to come to you, searched intently and with the greatest care, trying to find out the time and circumstances to which the Spirit of Christ in them was pointing when he predicted the suffering of Christ and the glories that would follow. It was revealed to them that they were not serving themselves but you, when they spoke of the things that have now been told you by those who have preached the gospel to you by the Holy Spirit sent from heaven. (I Peter 1:10-12)

Peter informs us that all prophecy involved God and the inspiration of the Holy Spirit. (II Peter 1:20-21) This truth was confirmed by Jesus, who taught that the entire Old Testament is God's Word. Jesus said that He did not come to abolish the Law or Prophets, but rather to fulfill both. (Matthew 5:17) Jesus often quoted the Hebrew Bible, stressing the inspiration of its words and the truths that they convey. He also stated that the Scriptures cannot be broken, meaning that they stand forever. (Matthew 22:29; John 10:34-35)

It is interesting that, while Peter sometimes had his differences with Paul, he believed that Paul's epistles to the churches were inspired by God. Peter said, "Paul's letters contain some things that are hard to understand, which ignorant and unstable people distort, as they do other Scriptures, to their own destruction." (II Peter 3:16) It is apparent that the apostles understood both the Hebrew Scriptures and their own writings to be inspired by God. Unlike people today, whose writings expound upon God's Word, the apostles were directed and inspired by the Holy Spirit to record what God directly communicated to them.

Our view of biblical inspiration influences our understanding and translation of the Scriptures and how they apply to our lives. Literalists not only adhere to biblical inerrancy, but some of them believe that God dictated every word to the writers. People even suggest that the Lord provided the punctuation, and that the Scriptures apply to us exactly as they did to people thousands of years ago. If we were to employ this belief, we would still be sacrificing animals, obeying ancient health laws, and prohibiting women from speaking in church. We may even believe that we can handle venomous snakes or consume poison without the fear of death. (Mark 16:17-18) These statements may sound extreme, but there are literalists who engage in some of these practices.

There is a more reasonable understanding of inspiration and inerrancy that is held by many Christians. It states that biblical inerrancy only relates to scripture that speaks to our salvation and Christian formation. In other words, while all the Scriptures are inspired, not all passages have equal importance. Also, rather than the theory, which claims that God dictated every word to the writers, this view believes that the writers used their own words and style to convey God's truths. With this approach, questions may surface as to which portions of the Bible are not applicable today; however, this can be resolved by employing reason and cultural understanding.

THE SACRAMENTS

The sacraments of the Church are another area where we find differences among Christians. Sacraments are formal rites that Christians believe were instituted by Christ and the early Church as a means of grace. The Roman Catholic Church practices seven sacraments, which are: baptism, confirmation, the Eucharist, penance, extreme unction (anointing the sick and dying), orders (clergy ordination) and marriage. Most Protestant denominations only embrace the Eucharist and baptism, believing that they are the only rites commanded by Jesus. Some Christians do not practice any sacrament, believing that they were never intended for the generations that followed the apostles. Others believe that an emphasis upon the sacraments may overshadow more important spiritual truths and practices. For example, to rely upon the sacraments as a path to salvation and spiritual formation may diminish the need to strive for holiness through faith, personal devotions, study and prayer. We will focus upon the Eucharist and baptism, which are the sacraments that are most familiar to people.

The Eucharist

The Eucharist, which is also known as the sacrament of Holy Communion, is a practiced rite in most Christian denominations. Some churches claim that this sacrament is necessary for one's spiritual life. In the Roman Catholic Church, the Eucharist is indispensable to the worship experience. There are also Protestant churches that believe Holy Communion is an essential part of worship. In Protestant churches this often depends upon denominational influences and a pastor's understanding of the Scriptures.

The three primary beliefs relating to Holy Communion are *transubstantiation, sacramental union,* and the *memorial view. Transubstantiation*, which is held by the Roman Catholic Church, is the belief that the wine and host literally change to the Blood and Body of Christ. Because it is believed that priests are in apostolic succession, they have been given the grace to initiate this miracle during the mass. The transformation of the elements is based upon the words of Christ when He referred to the Passover meal as His Body and Blood. Without providing an explanation, the apostle John recorded the following words of Jesus:

> I tell you the truth, unless you eat the flesh of the Son of Man and drink his blood, you have no life in you. Whoever eats my flesh and drinks my blood has eternal life, and I will raise him up at the last day. For my flesh is real food, and my blood is real drink. Whoever eats my flesh and drinks my blood remains in me and I in him. Just as the living Father sent me, and I live because of the Father, so the one who feeds on me will live because of me. This is the bread that came down from heaven. Our forefathers ate manna and died, but he who feeds on this bread will live forever. (John 6:53-58; I Corinthians 11:17-34)

Unlike other teachings, when Jesus spoke in figurative and symbolic language to explain God's truths, the Roman Catholic Church believes in the literal interpretation of these words. Because *Transubstantiation* miraculously changes the elements to the Body and Blood of Christ, what remains after administering the sacrament is stored with reverence in a consecrated place in the church. The continuous need for the sacrament is emphasized, for it is a channel for the forgiveness and grace that is necessary for salvation. To neglect the Eucharist is to reject the grace that God makes available through the sacrament.

The Lutheran Church understands the Eucharist as a *Sacramental Union,* in which Jesus' Body and Blood are believed to be *in, with, and under* the bread and wine. Unlike the Roman Catholic view, which states that the elements are changed, Lutherans claim that the Body and Blood of Christ miraculously coexist with the elements. It is Jesus' words given by the pastor that brings about this sacramental union during the worship service. According to this belief, the recipient is also receiving the Body and Blood of our Savior.

Most Protestants adhere to the *Memorial View* of Holy Communion, meaning that the sacrament brings us into a spiritual union with Christ, in which we reflect upon His sacrificial love. The elements are a graphic reminder of the price that was paid for our forgiveness and salvation. Our Savior knew that without this sacrament, people would seldom contemplate His selfless act of love. When we participate in the Eucharist we are moved to confession, thanksgiving and praise. This brings us closer to Jesus, igniting our faith and commitment. It also brings us closer to one another, for we are all united in one Spirit and share the same hope that is exemplified in the sacrament. While other views of the Eucharist exist in the Christian Church, these three provide us with a basic understanding of the sacrament.

Baptism

Water baptism, as a preparation for the ministry of Jesus, began with John the Baptist. John's mission was to confront people with their sins, stressing their need for God's forgiveness. (Matthew 3:5-6) John told the people that, while he baptized with water for repentance, one would follow him who would baptize with the Holy Spirit and fire. (Matthew 3:11-12) With John's baptism, the water was symbolically used to signify the inner cleansing that comes through repentance. His ministry was to prepare people's hearts for Jesus' message of forgiveness and salvation. (Acts 2:38-41)

To satisfy divine righteousness and to identify with humanity, Jesus allowed John to baptize Him. John initially resisted, stating that he instead needed to be baptized by Jesus. Our Savior's baptism reveals the significance of the sacrament, with Jesus being the example for His followers. When Jesus was baptized, God confirmed His divinity. This was an important affirmation for John the Baptist, who was martyred for his faith and preaching ministry. It was our Lord's baptism and, His command that all believers be baptized, that has given the Church this sacrament. Since the first century, people from all over the world have been baptized in the name of the Father, Son, and the Holy Spirit.

Luke provides us with a clear picture of water baptism during the time of the apostles, revealing that people were baptized as a profession of their faith. The water was symbolic of an inner cleansing and spiritual renewal that came through the work of the Holy Spirit. The baptism was a constant reminder of one's profession of faith and their promise to walk in the teachings of Christ. It was also a public statement that spoke to the hearts of witnesses, leading them to examine their lives and look to Jesus for salvation.

Jesus did not command that infants should be baptized, but the mention of entire households receiving the sacrament may have included children. (Acts 16:11-34) It is obvious that baptism was intended for those who understood the Gospel message and could willfully receive Jesus Christ into their lives. Although infant baptism is not rooted in biblical teachings, some theologians justify it by making references to Jesus' desire to bless children, and how He spoke about their innocent faith and place in God's kingdom. While these truths are noteworthy, they must not be used as a basis for infant baptism.

Many denominations have adopted infant baptism, to the exclusion of being baptized as an adult. Some Christians even believe that infant baptism is necessary for spiritual regeneration, specifically the forgiveness of original sin. Simply stated, there is no biblical truth for this belief. In fact, to believe this could bring parents great distress if their child were to die before being baptized. God's love will never condemn a child who dies before reaching the age of accountability, which comes through understanding, conviction and the exercise of free will. While some people make judgments in this area, only God knows when accountability becomes a reality.

I believe in infant baptism as a dedication of children and a parental statement of faith, in which there is a promise to raise the child in the Church. Although parents serve as the primary Christian example for their children, the Church has a responsibility to support and pray for all children. This should be communicated during the sacrament, with church members making a promise to love and encourage children in the faith. While infant baptism is a parental act, adult baptism is our profession of faith before God and witnesses. The first baptism begins a life that is supported by parents and the Church, and the second one confirms our faith and the desire to commit our lives to Jesus Christ.

Parents who desire to have their children baptized must understand the meaning of the sacrament and the promises that they are making before God and witnesses. There should be instructions given, along with ample time for parents to pray about their decision. Without this preparation, it is just a ritual that is performed out of tradition and a sense of duty. It is the responsibility of the Church to educate its members in all areas of doctrine, and this includes the sacraments. Many people who dedicate their children to God do not keep their promises. In some cases, a child's baptism is the last time that parents bring them to church.

I grew up in the Lutheran Church and was baptized as an infant. Fortunately, my parents kept their promise to God, and I was raised in the Church. At the age of thirteen I was confirmed, and I continued attending church until enlisting in the

Navy. After that point my attendance was sporadic, until I was in my thirties. During my first year as a pastor, I felt led to be baptized as an adult. During an evening service another pastor baptized me, with the congregation witnessing my profession of faith. It was an experience that I will never forget. Everyone should prayerfully consider adult baptism, as it is a blessing for both the individual and a congregation.

While serving as a state prison chaplain, I baptized approximately three hundred inmates over a period of seven years. The baptisms were through immersion, with both prisoners and staff members as witnesses. These were men who attended weekly Bible studies and were committed Christians, often helping other inmates with their problems and spiritual issues. Before their immersion, each person gave a brief testimony relating how they received Jesus as their Savior. During these services one could sense the power of the Holy Spirit moving upon the hearts of those in attendance. While some of these individuals have obviously not kept their baptismal promise, the seeds of salvation were planted through the sacrament.

— CHAPTER TWO —

Crucifixion of Jesus

The incarnation of Jesus Christ was the manifestation of God to a lost and dying world. Jesus came to us with the message of forgiveness, reconciliation, and eternal life. His mission was one of love, calling us to repentance and faith. The Father knew that the ministry of His Son would result in His death, and it is within this understanding that we find the essence of salvation. God predestined salvation for those who, in faith, would receive Jesus Christ and His atoning sacrifice on the cross. Like the lambs that were sacrificed under Mosaic Law as sin offerings, Jesus is the Lamb of God whose death brings forgiveness and spiritual renewal. He died a sinner's death, which means that He was separated from the Father as He bore our sins.

The death of Jesus Christ brought the light of His resurrection, without which there would be no hope for humanity. Jesus assures us that because He lives, we also shall live eternally in His presence. (John 11:25-26) Our Savior's resurrection is the proof of His claims and promises, a reality that is affirmed by the Spirit who lives within us. For those who live in faith, death is the door that brings everlasting peace and glory.

SYMBOL OF THE CROSS

Prior to the Christian era, we find the cross being used as both a heathen sign and an emblem related to some manner of nature worship. Etchings of different types of cross symbols have been found on Phoenician monuments, buildings in Nineveh, and Egyptian art. These symbols have also been seen on the vestments of Egyptian priests. The swastika, which is another form of cross dating back to Neolithic times, has been found in early art. It is believed that the swastika was an ancient religious symbol. As we know, this form of cross was used by the Third Reich and Nazi Germany. Today, it is regarded as a symbol for evil and anti-Semitism. While it is difficult to know the cultural and religious meanings of these symbols, for Christianity the cross represents God's sacrificial love and our salvation.

It is not known when the cross became a universal symbol for the Christian faith, but it may have been used as early as the late first century. If so, it is doubtful that it was widely recognized as a communicative symbol for Christianity. During those early years the cross remained a repulsive image for most people. There is evidence that it became a Christian symbol during the reign of Constantine the Great, who ruled the Roman Empire from 306-337 A.D. He was the first emperor to adopt the cross as an ensign, with coins bearing its form, along with monograms of himself or Christ. The image of our suffering Savior was added to the cross, forming the crucifix in the sixth century. During Rome's civil war, Constantine saw the vision of a cross, which he interpreted as a sign of his victory. The victory did come when he defeated Maxentius near Rome.

Constantine issued the Edict of Milan in 313 A.D., which proclaimed religious tolerance throughout his empire. In 323 A.D., when he became the sole ruler of the Roman Empire, the Edict of Milan was extended to the Eastern half of the Empire. The three hundred years of Christian persecution had finally come to an end. Then, in 330 A.D. Constantine established Christianity as the State religion. This unprecedented and bold move was probably influenced by his mother, Empress Helena, who had been converted to Christianity.

Constantine was deeply moved by what he saw as the victory-bearing *Sign of the Cross*, and he embarked on a search to locate the actual cross of Jesus. He sent his mother to Jerusalem on this mission, and through her interviews she was informed that the cross was buried at the site of an ancient temple. As a result, she ordered that the temple be destroyed and the area excavated. It was there that a tomb, believed to be the one that held Jesus, was discovered. Near this site there were three crosses, execution nails, and a board with the inscription *Ordered by Pilate*. Although this location is presently within the old city of Jerusalem, during the time of Christ it was beyond the city limits. This is significant because we know that the executions took place beyond the city walls at a place called *Golgotha*, which means the *place of the skull*. I visited this location, which is where the Church of the Holy Sepulcher is now located.

As a symbol, the cross has taken many cultural forms, but for Christians it represents the universal Church and God's offer of salvation through Jesus Christ. It is a symbol found in ecclesiastical rites, processions, art and architecture. Christians view the symbol of the empty cross as a sign of the risen Christ, who gained victory over death. The cross that once held the body of Jesus is now empty. We worship a risen Savior who promises to give us the same victory. But whether the symbol is an empty cross or one that emphasizes the suffering Jesus, the message remains the same. To contemplate the cross of Jesus Christ is to open up a channel for God's grace to flow into our lives. No other symbol more clearly reveals the heart of God and the needs of humanity. What was once a cruel instrument of death is now a universal sign of God's love and our hope in Jesus Christ.

ANCIENT CRUCIFIXIONS

During the time of Christ people were executed on wood stakes or various forms of a cross, which included those in the shape of an **X** and an upright with a crossbar. Some crossbars were formed like a **T**, while other cross members were lowered, allowing for an inscription above the victim's head. This type, which is known as the Latin cross, was apparently used in our Savior's execution. The victims were either tied or nailed to these instruments of death, which were intended to humiliate and prolong suffering. The very thought of a cross brought fear among the people, especially if they were a defeated enemy and under foreign occupation. Such was the situation with the Jews, who were under Roman authority. History reveals that crucifixion was used by the Egyptians (Genesis 40:19), as well as the Persians and Carthaginians. After his conquest over Tyre, Alexander the Great crucified over two thousand Tyrians who resisted his invasion.

Crucifixion was widely used by the Romans, with exemption only given to Roman citizens. The apostle Paul, although a Jew, was a Roman citizen. Instead of being crucified, he was beheaded during the reign of Nero. In comparison to crucifixion, this type of death was viewed as an act of mercy. Prior to being crucified the victims were flogged, almost to the point of death. This was done with a whip of leather straps that were laced with sharp pieces of bone or metal balls. The scourging was administered over the person's entire body, ripping through the flesh, causing extensive bleeding and contusions.

The executions took place in full view of the public, which served as a warning to the people. While most of the victims died within three or four days, there were instances when they survived longer. Sometimes the criminal was placed on the cross while it was on the ground, fastened to it by ropes or nails, and then raised with it as the upright was dropped into a prepared hole or socket. In other instances, the person was attached to the crossbar, which was then raised with ropes to its proper place on the upright. It was also a practice to raise the body with the use of a ladder and then fastened it to a cross that was already in an upright position. The nails used in Roman crucifixions were approximately six inches long and were either driven through the palms of the hands or the wrists. If the nails were driven through the palms and there was no platform for the feet, the weight of the body could result in the nails ripping through the hands. Nailing the feet to a platform was intended to limit a person's movement and prolong the suffering. Victims would try to stand as long as possible, but once the legs cramped and exhaustion occurred the body would slump, causing the lungs to collapse.

As part of the punishment, the sufferer was sometimes forced to carry his own cross or crossbar to the place of crucifixion. It was not unusual, especially after the scourging, for the victim to fall under its weight. The Scriptures reveal that, while walking through the streets of Jerusalem, Jesus fell under the weight of His cross. When this happened, the guards placed it on a man by the name of Simon. (Luke 23:26) Visitors traveling to Israel are able to walk the path that Jesus took on the way to His execution. This route is known as the Via Dolorosa, which means *Way of Grief* or *Way of Suffering*.

Before being nailed to the cross the Romans removed the clothing of the condemned person. If the clothing had any value it was kept by the guards. The Gospels record that the soldiers divided up Jesus' clothing and cast lots for His seamless tunic. While most criminals were poor and their clothing valueless, there were certainly individuals who came from a higher standard of living. The removal of one's clothing may seem insignificant in terms of their torture, but it was nonetheless degrading for both the victim and his family members.

Since victims of crucifixion could linger on the cross for three or more days, the guards would often hasten death by breaking the criminal's legs. The Jews sometimes requested this, particularly if the Sabbath was approaching. When the person died, their body was often left to decay on the cross or taken to the city dump to be burned. Bodies that were left to rot were devoured by birds and other animals. Before taking their last breath the victims experienced exposure, shock, dehydration and asphyxiation.

HEBREW SACRIFICIAL SYSTEM

History records ancient civilizations practicing both animal and human sacrifices. While it is impossible to know the depth of their reasoning, sacrifices of a religious nature seem to have focused upon relationships with one or more deity. These offerings were primarily intended to appease a particular god, establish some manner of reconciliation, or serve as a channel to receive divine favor. Some of them were offerings of praise and thanksgiving for gifts, which were understood to have come from above. Although the study of Hebrew sacrifices is complex and requires considerable study, it is important to outline their purpose and how they relate to the death of Christ. During the time of the patriarchs, sacrifices were often spontaneous responses of reverence and trust in God. Like other civilizations, they also encompassed elements of praise and thanksgiving. It was under Mosaic Law that mandated offerings were established.

The first recorded sacrifices in the Bible were those of Cain and Abel (Genesis 4:3-5) and Noah after the flood. (Genesis 8:20) The attempted sacrifice of Isaac by Abraham is the only mention of human sacrifice. According to the Scriptures, the Lord, who prevented Isaac's death, had put Abraham's faith to the test. (Genesis 22:1-13) Job offered burnt offerings for each of his children, believing that they had sinned and cursed God in their hearts. This became Job's regular custom and an indication that early sacrifices were also connected with the forgiveness of sins. (Job 1:4-5) Under Mosaic Law the Lord set into motion a system in which unblemished animals were sacrificed, with their blood sprinkled upon the altar. This may seem cruel, but we should note that portions of the animal's remains were given to the priests, temple workers, and families for food. This, of course, depended upon the type of sacrifice that was offered up to God. Sacrifices normally included animals such as lambs, goats, cattle, and rams for people who could afford them. Those who were poor were permitted to sacrifice pigeons or other acceptable animals.

Under the law sacrifices became a covenant duty, the details of which were given to Moses by God. The law required five types of sacrifices, with the burnt offerings and sin offerings being most significant. Burnt offerings began in the wilderness and were regularly performed. (Exodus 29:38-42; Numbers 28:9-11; 29:39) This offering embodied the concept of *surrender to God*, as well as an emphasis upon *obedience* and *holy living*. According to the law, sinners were not permitted to offer themselves up to the Lord without a sinless and perfect intercessor. As such, unblemished animals became substitutes for the imperfections and sinfulness of the people. It was a symbol of transference when someone placed their hand on the head of an unblemished animal that was about to be sacrificed. These offerings were a continuous reminder of a person's sins and God's holiness.

The shedding of the animal's blood represented the blood of the person or, in some cases, the nation of Israel. In biblical times and throughout history blood has been representative of both life and death. This is easy to understand because the receiving of blood gives life, while the loss of blood takes it away. The blood that was sprinkled upon the altar was symbolic of the life and soul of the people. In essence, it communicated the offering up of one's life to God. The blood shedding also spoke to the forgiveness of sins, for without the shedding of blood there is no forgiveness. The author of Hebrews wrote, "When Moses had proclaimed every commandment of the law to all the people, he took the blood of the calves, together with water, scarlet wool and branches of hyssop, and sprinkled the scroll and all the people....without the shedding of blood there is no forgiveness." (Hebrews 9:19-22) Since the fall of humanity, the penalty for sin is both physical and spiritual death. However, since we will all die physically, the focus here is spiritual death, which is separation from God. When Jesus shed His blood on the cross, He paid the penalty for our sins, which has reconciled us to the Father and granted us spiritual life. We, who were once dead in our transgressions, are now alive in Jesus Christ.

The *burnt offering* was considered to be the most important Hebrew sacrifice. It required that the entire animal be consumed by fire. This complete consumption, along with the shedding of the animal's blood, provides a window into the death of Jesus Christ. The Lord gave Moses instructions for this sacrifice, which are found in the first chapter of Leviticus. The *burnt offerings,* along with the *sin offerings,* served as a channel for the forgiveness of sins. (Leviticus 4:2-3,13-14, 22-23, 35; 5:20) They also had Messianic significance in that they pointed to the ultimate sacrifice of Jesus Christ. As the *Lamb of God*, Jesus was the unblemished sacrifice who was offered up for the world. When John the Baptist saw Jesus coming to him to be baptized, he said, "Look, the Lamb of God, who takes away the sins of the world." (John 1:29)

God was not pleased with the result of animal sacrifices because they became mechanical rituals that lacked redemptive power. What was meant to bring the Israelites closer to the Lord and promote holy living, became a heartless system that lacked repentance and praise. The author of Hebrews wrote about this, saying, "When Christ came into the world, sacrifice and offering you did not desire, but a body you prepared for me; with burnt offerings and sin offerings you were not pleased." (Hebrews 10:5-6) Jesus became both our *burnt and sin offerings* before God. Referring to Jesus, Paul told the Corinthians that the *Passover Lamb* had been sacrificed. (I Corinthians 5:7) In his second letter to the congregation, he said, "God made him who had no sin to be sin for us, so that in him we might become the righteousness of God." (II Corinthians 5:21) The author of Hebrews wrote that "Jesus appeared once for all at the end of the ages to do away with sin by the sacrifice of himself. Just as man is destined to die once, and after that to face judgment, so Christ was sacrificed once to take away the sins of many people." (Hebrews 9:26-28)

The death of Christ is also our death, meaning that it is the death of the sinful nature. Paul assured the Romans of this truth, saying, "For we know that our old self was crucified with him, so that the body of sin might be done away with, that we no longer be slaves to sin – because anyone who has died has been freed from sin." (Romans 6:6-7) It is through the power of the cross and the indwelling Spirit that we have victory over the sinful nature. In Jesus Christ we have become new creatures who desire to serve God and one another. Those born of God have been baptized in the Spirit and are no longer slaves to sin. They are set free to live as God intends and to follow the righteous path that is set before them. Followers of Jesus are a priesthood of believers, who are called to be servants through the sacrificial offering up of their lives. Like our Savior, we are to offer our bodies *as living sacrifices*, holy and pleasing to God. According to the apostle Paul, this is true worship. (Romans 12:1; Hebrews 13:15)

OLD TESTAMENT PROPHECY

Although there are many Messianic Scriptures in the Hebrew Bible, it is important we examine those that clearly relate to the crucifixion of Christ. What follows is not an exhaustive recording, primarily because I believe that some passages accepted by others are questionable. The earliest prophecy that most Christian scholars agree upon is found in the first book of the Bible, whose authorship is attributed to Moses.

Genesis 3:15 (1450-1420 B.C.)

I will put enmity between you and the woman, and between your offspring and hers; he will crush your head, and you will strike his heel.

Christian scholars have researched and pondered this passage for centuries and, while there are some different understandings, the essential message remains. This is not the case with Jewish theologians, who frame these words within a different context. However, for the Christian Church this brief verse speaks to the humble intervention of God into our world. It is also the first revelation of what would be a continuing battle between good and evil. This verse contains the Advent of Christ, His crucifixion, and His victory over the power of Satan. The apostle Paul assured the Colossians that on the cross our Savior triumphed over the powers of evil. (Colossians 2:14-15) This triumph will ultimately result in the final destruction of Satan and all evil forces. In Revelation we learn that Satan and his followers will be thrown into the lake of fire, where they will be tormented forever. (Revelation 20:10)

The spiritual warfare between Satan and his offspring and the offspring of the *woman* is understood in different ways. Some biblical students understand the woman to be Eve, but if we interpret this statement in light of Jesus' incarnation, it must refer to the *Virgin Birth*. Biblical genealogies are always given through the male, which makes this prophecy unique. To mention a woman's lineage in a strictly enforced patriarchal system was simply not acceptable. Therefore, this reference obviously refers to the miraculous birth of Jesus through the power of the Holy Spirit. Some theologians seem hesitant in naming *Mary* as the *woman* in this prophecy, but it was Mary whom God chose to receive the seed of His Son.

The *enmity* between Satan and the woman is the hatred and spiritual warfare between the seeds of good and evil that will continue until the Second Advent of Jesus Christ. (Galatians 3:16) It is a battle between the followers of Christ and those who reject him as Lord and Savior. The world consists of those who love God and those who live in sin. Jesus taught that He did not come into the world to bring peace, not even within one's household. He stressed that within one's own family there would be believers and those who will reject His

Gospel message. (Matthew 10:34-39) The apostle John even warns Christians about becoming lukewarm in their faith and commitment. To the church in Philadelphia, he wrote, "I know your deeds, that you are neither cold nor hot. I wish you were either one or the other! So, because you are lukewarm – neither hot nor cold – I am going to spit you out of my mouth." (Revelation 3:15-16) John also said, "No one who is born of God will continue to sin, because God's seed remains in him; he cannot go on sinning because he has been born of God. This is how we know who the children of God are and who the children of the devil are: Anyone who does not do what is right is not a child of God; neither is anyone who does not love his brother." (I John 3:8-10) John's teachings stress that Jesus came to destroy the works of the devil. Those who have received Christ into their lives know how their spiritual birth has changed their life and relationships. Christians are to love all people, regardless of the circumstances. However, this is not to say that there will not be relational difficulties. To love others does not mean that we compromise our faith and commitment to the Lord.

There are primarily two interpretations for the second part of this scripture. Through the fall of humanity Satan dealt Jesus a bruising assault, but at the cross Jesus crushed Satan's head. While the former can be understood as a wound that requires healing, the latter reflects a mortal blow that will ultimately result in death. The *striking of the heel* is the wound that Jesus received on the cross when the nails were driven through his feet. Satan may wound us in this life, but we are assured of victory in Jesus Christ.

Isaiah 53 (780-695 B.C.)

The early church attributed this writing to the prophet Isaiah, but some critics believe that this chapter and subsequent ones were written by a different author. If this is true, then the date of this chapter is probably earlier. But regardless of the exact date, the importance and accuracy of this prophecy stands firm. This writing details the suffering and death of Jesus, as well as His resurrection. It also provides the reason for His crucifixion. In penetrating metaphors, we see a Savior who willingly offered up His life for the sins of the world. Jesus did not lose His life but rather gave it for the ungodly, including the worst of sinners. This prophecy, which is the fulfillment of Genesis 3:15, is the most graphic of all Messianic prophecies. It is also at the very heart of our redemption. Although it communicates painful images that pierce our hearts, it is a clear message of God's love and our hope in Jesus Christ. These are Isaiah's words:

> Who has believed our message, and to whom has the arm of the Lord been revealed? (2) He grew up before him like a tender shoot, and like a root out of dry ground. He had no beauty or majesty to attract us to him, nothing in his appearance that we should desire him. (3) He was despised and rejected by men, a man of sorrows, and familiar with suffering. Like one from whom men hide their faces he was despised, and we esteemed him not. (4) Surely, he took up our infirmities and carried our sorrows, yet we considered him stricken by God, smitten by him, and af-

flicted. (5) But he was pierced for our transgressions, he was crushed for our iniquities; the punishment that brought us peace was upon him, and by his wounds we are healed. (6) We all, like sheep, have gone astray, each of us has turned to his own way; and the Lord has laid on him the iniquity of us all. (7) He was oppressed and afflicted, yet he did not open his mouth; he was led like a lamb to the slaughter, and as a sheep before her shearers is silent, so he did not open his mouth. (8) By oppression and judgment, he was taken away. And who can speak of his descendants? For he was cut off from the land of the living; for the transgressions of my people, he was stricken. (9) He was assigned a grave with the wicked, and with the rich in his death, though he had done no violence, nor was any deceit in his mouth. (10) Yet it was the Lord's will to crush him and cause him to suffer, and though the Lord makes his life a guilt offering, he will see his offspring and prolong his days, and the will of the Lord will prosper in his hand. (11) After the suffering of his soul, he will see the light of life and be satisfied; by his knowledge my righteous servant will justify many, and he will bear their iniquities. (12) Therefore, I will give him a portion among the great, and he will divide the spoils with the strong, because he poured out his life unto death, and was numbered with the transgressors. For he bore the sin of many and made intercession for the transgressors.

As we progress through this prophecy, we gain insight into our Savior's suffering and why He entered our world. It begins with a far-reaching question. *Who has believed our message, and to whom has the arm of the Lord been revealed?* We should first note the word <u>our</u> which is found in this question. This is unquestionably a reference to the Godhead acting in unity. The *arm of the Lord* speaks to God's intervention reaching down to us through the life, death, and resurrection of Christ. But how many people, past and present, have accepted the message of salvation? The answer to this question, although obvious, is left for the reader to answer.

In verses two and three we gain some insight into our Savior's development, physical appearance, and humanity's response to Him. The statement *He grew up before him* suggests the Father's presence and guidance throughout Jesus' developing years. There was never a time when we do not see an intimate communion between Jesus and God the Father, including His childhood years as recorded by Luke. Jesus grew up as a *tender shoot*, meaning that He was a child of compassion, humility and innocence. These developing traits later defined His adult life and ministry, serving as an example to His disciples and others.

While many artists have painted Christ with handsome features, including long flowing hair and a manicured beard, Isaiah reveals something quite different. He informs us that there was *nothing in his appearance that would attract us to him.* In fact, Jesus lacked beauty and majesty. By society's standards he was not viewed in a positive light. He simply did not pass the test of a charismatic and assertive Messiah who would restore power and dignity to the people. There was also nothing special about His lineage or upbringing. The people rejected Him, not believing His claims or authority. If this were not enough, Isaiah tells us that He was even despised by some people.

Jesus was *a man of sorrows and familiar with suffering*, who was cast aside by those whom He came to save from sin and death. But instead of His sorrow being for Himself, it was for those who refused to respond to His love and forgiveness. Parents of unsaved children know the sorrow that comes when thinking about their child's plight without the Lord in their life. Jesus also felt the pain of God's lost children. He lamented over Jerusalem, saying, "O Jerusalem, Jerusalem, you who kill the prophets and stone those sent to you. How often I have longed to gather your children together as a hen gathers her chicks under her wings, but you were not willing. Look, your house is left desolate." (Matthew 23:37-38) For God's Son to give His life for His enemies and be rejected by them, reveals a level of suffering that is beyond our comprehension.

Verse four reads, *"We considered him stricken by God, smitten by him, and afflicted."* This reflects a belief that Jesus was being punished for His own sins. Such thinking was common at that time. An example of this are the responses to Job's suffering by his friends. This belief would especially be true if Jesus were a false Messiah and guilty of blasphemy. Even today, there is the belief that God punishes people every time they step out of line. I have often experienced this negativity in my ministries. Some individuals have concluded that every disease is a punishment from God for sin. They fail to grasp or accept the grace that flows through the cross of Jesus Christ. This is not to assume that our sins will not have destructive results, for we tend to reap what we have sown. But it is abhorrent to equate disease or any other misfortune as a punishment from God.

Verse five is at the heart of Isaiah's prophecy, for it directly focuses upon the crucifixion of Jesus. When reading this passage, we shudder at the thought of our Lord's body being pierced with nails and hanging on a cross. Added to this, is that He died a sinner's death, being separated from the Father and Holy Spirit. Clearly stated, when Jesus was crucified death took place within the Godhead. To think that God did this for the worst of sinners forces us to look at ourselves. Isaiah tells us that Jesus was literally pierced for our sins, and it is through His suffering and death that we receive forgiveness, spiritual healing, and reconciliation.

Verses six and seven affirm that no person is without sin; therefore, the atoning sacrifice of Christ is universal. Verse six reads, *"We all, like sheep, have gone astray, each of us has turned to his own way."* The apostle John said, "If we claim we have not sinned, we make him out to be a liar and his word has no place in our lives." (I John 1:10) Paul emphasized that "all have sinned and fall short of the glory of God, and are justified freely by his grace that came by Christ Jesus." (Romans 3:23-25) Isaiah addressed both our sins and righteousness when he said, "All of us have become like one who is unclean, and all our righteous acts are like filthy rags; we all shrivel up like a leaf, and like the wind our sins sweep us away." (Isaiah 64:6-7) Even though Jesus was guiltless and without sin, *"he was led like a lamb to the slaughter."* He was passive and completely surrendered to the Father's will, knowing that it was saving grace for the world.

Verse eight reads, *"And who can speak of his descendants? For he was cut off from the land of the living; for the transgressions of my people, he was stricken."* A premature death often eliminates the possibility of having children, but Jesus' descendants are those who are spiritually quickened by the Holy Spirit, and they come from every nation. What started out with twelve faithful disciples is now an everlasting kingdom that has conquered sin and death for those who place their trust in Jesus Christ.

Jesus was crucified with two criminals and, if it were not for the intervention of two wealthy men, His body would probably have been discarded with the criminals. But Nicodemus and Joseph of Arimathea received permission from Pontius Pilate to bury our Lord. They were believers in Jesus and wanted His body to be respected according to Jewish custom. Nicodemus brought with him a mixture of myrrh and aloes to anoint the body. He and Joseph took our Savior down from the cross and placed His body in Joseph's personal tomb. This fulfilled the prophecy stating that *"he was assigned a grave with the wicked, and with a rich man in his death."* In accordance with God's will, the compassion of these two men provided the foundation for Jesus' resurrection.

Who can begin to understand the depth of Jesus' suffering? But in verses ten and eleven we learn of the joyful satisfaction that He would experience after His resurrection. Isaiah wrote, *"He will see the light of life and be satisfied."* Jesus would not only realize the salvation of souls, but the Father would *prolong His days* on earth after He was brought back to life. It was divine providence that Jesus' followers see Him for the forty days prior to His ascension, for it enabled Him to prove His deity and reinforce the truths of the Gospel. It was also an encouragement for His apostles and others for the challenges that awaited them.

The words "*by* his *knowledge my righteous servant will justify many*" should be understood as the truth and authority that Jesus possesses to forgive sins. As both the Logos and our intercessor, Jesus brings life where there was death. Our Savior is explicit when He says that no one comes to the Father except through Him. Because of His atoning sacrifice, the Father has exalted Him to rule and judge the nations. Isaiah prophesied, "*I will give him a portion among the great, and he will divide the spoils with the strong.*" In this verse Jesus is compared to a warrior king, which is an analogy that the people could understand. It was the victor in battle who divided the spoils of war. The Lord's battle, however, continues to be against the evil forces that seek to destroy us. This passage affirms that through His sacrifice we share in His victory. We are the "*strong*" in faith and commitment who will receive the eternal rewards that Jesus promises.

King David, who wrote at least 75 of the 150 psalms, is the author of the Messianic Scriptures that follow. They were written during his reign in the tenth century B.C.

Psalm 16:9-11 (cf. Acts 2:31)

Therefore, my heart is glad and my tongue rejoices; my body will also rest secure, because you will not abandon me to the grave, nor will you let your Holy One see decay. You have made known to me the path of life; you will fill me with joy in your presence, with eternal pleasures at your right hand.

The body of Jesus was not burned, nor did it experience decay. On the third day He was brought back to life. God did not allow His Son to remain in the sepulcher. The *path of life* refers to Jesus' resurrection and the results of His atoning sacrifice, which filled Him with joy.

Psalm 68:18-19 (cf. Acts 1:9)

When you ascend on high, you led captives in your train; you received gifts from men, even from the rebellious – that you, O Lord God, might dwell there. Praise be to the Lord, to God our Savior, who daily bears our burdens.

The words *ascend on high* refer to the ascension of Christ. Jesus came to set the captives free, meaning everyone living under the influence of sin. Freedom comes through following Jesus. At a synagogue in Galilee, Jesus stood up in front of the people and read Isaiah's prophecy, saying, "The Spirit of the Lord is on me, because he has anointed me to preach good news to the poor. He has sent me to proclaim freedom for the prisoners and recovery of sight for the blind, to release the oppressed, to proclaim the year of the Lord's favor." (Isaiah 61:1-2; John 8:32, 36) Even though Jesus bore our sins on the cross, this psalm tells us that He *daily bears our burdens.*

Psalm 22:1, 13-18 (cf. Luke 23:34; John 19:23-24)

My God, my God, why have you forsaken me?....Roaring lions tearing their prey, open their mouths wide against me. I am poured out like water, and all my bones are out of joint. My heart has turned to wax; it has melted away within me. My strength is dried up like a potsherd, and my tongue sticks to the roof of my mouth; you lay me in the dust of death. Dogs have surrounded me; a band of evil men have encircled me. They have pierced my hands and my feet. I can count all my bones; people stare and gloat over me. They divide my garments among them and cast lots for my clothing.

Realizing the Father's absence, we hear the agonizing cry of Jesus. The words reflect the depth of His isolation and suffering as He bore our sins. Everything that is echoed in this psalm occurred at the crucifixion site. It even includes a reference to the guards dividing up His clothing and casting lots for His tunic. David provides powerful imagery that is difficult for us to emotionally process.

Psalm 34:20 (cf. John 19:36)

He protects all of his bones, not one of them will be broke.

Unlike other crucifixions in which the legs of the victims were sometimes broken to hasten death, not one of our Savior's bones was broken. When the soldiers came to Jesus, they discovered that He was already dead. After six hours on the cross Jesus offered up His spirit to the Father. What He came to do for humanity was completed. To be certain that Jesus was dead, a guard pierced His side with a spear. (John 19:33-34)

Psalm 69:21 (cf. Matthew 27:34; Mark 15:23; John 19:28-30)

They put gall in my food and gave me vinegar for my thirst.

The Gospels mention two occasions when Jesus was offered a liquid mixture to help dull His pain. Matthew states that it was wine mixed with gall. According to Mark it was wine mixed with myrrh. The apostle John informs us that someone soaked a sponge with wine vinegar, placed it on a stalk of hyssop plant, and lifted it to Jesus' lips. It would seem strange for a guard to do this, especially in light of the intended punishment and circumstances.

This may have been a common practice for those witnessing the executions.

Psalm 109:25 (cf. Matthew 27:39)

I am an object of scorn to my accusers; when they see me, they shake their heads.

This is a reference to the cruelty of the soldiers, religious leaders and others, who were gathered at our Savior's execution. To prove that He was the Son of God He was told to come down from the cross. They said, "If you are the king of the Jews, save yourself." Others cried out, "He saved others; let him save himself if he is the Christ of God, the Chosen One." Even a criminal who was crucified alongside of Jesus hurled out insults at Him. (Luke 23:35-39)

Isaiah 50:6-7 (cf. Matthew 27:27-31; John 19:1-3)

I offered my back to those who beat me, my cheeks to those who pulled out my beard; I did not hide my face from mocking and spitting. Because the Sovereign Lord helps me, I will not be disgraced. Therefore, I have set my face like flint, and I know I will not be put to shame.

Jesus stood firm in the midst of His suffering. This is communicated in the words *I have set my face like flint.* He knew that His crucifixion was God's will and that the results would bring glory to the Father. The *shame* that others attached to His crucifixion was the means through which sinners are reconciled to God.

Isaiah 52:14

There were many who were appalled at him – his appearance was so disfigured beyond that of any man and his form marred beyond human likeness.

This statement is shocking! It tells us that the beatings Jesus endured were so intense that they disfigured Him. To think that this preceded the agony of the crucifixion is incomprehensible. There is nothing that we can add to these words.

Daniel 9:24-26 (605-536 B.C.)

After the sixty-two 'sevens,' the Anointed One will be cut off and will have nothing. The people of the ruler who will come will destroy the city and the sanctuary. The end will come like a flood: War will continue till the end, and desolations have been decreed.

The symbolic numbers in verses twenty-four through twenty-six are difficult to interpret. This scripture, however, clearly addresses the Advent of Christ and his death. Verse twenty-four, not shown above, gives us insight into the purpose of Jesus' Advent, which was to *atone for wickedness, to bring everlasting righteousness and to seal up vision and prophecy.* In verse twenty-six we find the *Anointed One cut off,* meaning that He was put to death. Daniel also alludes to the destruction of Jerusalem, which occurred in 70 A.D. Jesus is the fulfillment of Hebrew prophecy, whose sacrificial death brought everlasting righteousness to all who believe in Him.

Zechariah 12:10 (520-518 B.C.)

And I will pour out on the house of David and the inhabitants of Jerusalem a spirit of grace and supplication. They will look on me, the one they have pierced, and they will mourn for him as one mourns for an only child.

According to Zechariah, people would come to realize that Jesus was their Messiah, and they would mourn over His death.

Many people believed in Christ after His resurrection and the preaching of the Gospel. Those who initially rejected His message were saddened by their previous disbelief and the suffering that Jesus endured.

Numbers 21:4-9 (Moses: 1450-1410 B.C., cf. John 3:14-16)

> They traveled from Mount Hor along the route to the Red Sea, to go around Edom. But the people grew impatient on the way; they spoke against God and against Moses, and said, "Why have you brought us up out of Egypt to die in the desert? There is no bread! There is no water! And we detest this miserable food!" Then the Lord sent venomous snakes among them; they bit the people and many Israelites died. The people came to Moses and said, "We sinned when we spoke against you. Pray that the Lord will take the snakes away from us." So, Moses prayed for the people. The Lord said to Moses, "Make a snake and put it up on a pole; anyone who was bitten can look at it and live." So, Moses made a bronze snake and put it up on a pole. Then when anyone was bitten by a snake and looked at the bronze snake, he lived.

What we find here is the Lord confronting the sins of the people, as well as testing their faith. Although this scripture may not be considered prophecy relating to the crucifixion, it is interesting that Jesus alluded to it when speaking to Nicodemus. Jesus wanted Nicodemus to understand that the Messiah's death was foretold by the prophets. Nicodemus was an educated leader and member of the Jewish Council, but he failed to comprehend how the death of Jesus was rooted in prophecy. Jesus said to Nicodemus, "Just as Moses lifted up the snake in the desert, so the Son of Man must be lifted up, that everyone who believes in him may have eternal life." (John 3:14-16; Acts 2:23-24)

Zechariah 11:12-13 (cf. Matthew 26:14-16; 27:3-10)

I told them, "If you think it best, give me my pay; but if not, keep it." So, they paid me thirty pieces of silver. And the Lord said to me, "Throw it to the potter – the handsome price at which they pierced me!" So, I took the thirty pieces of silver and threw them into the house of the Lord.

The chief priests paid Judas Iscariot thirty pieces of silver to deliver Jesus to them. When Judas received the money, he waited for an opportune time to betray Jesus. While our Savior was in the Garden of Gethsemane with His disciples, He was confronted by a large crowd armed with swords and clubs. They were sent by the chief priests and elders to take Jesus into custody. It was decided that Judas would identify Jesus by kissing Him. (Matthew 26:47-50) After Jesus was arrested and condemned, Judas became remorseful, for he realized that the Council was seeking to put Jesus to death. Judas tried to return the thirty pieces of silver to the chief priests and elders, but they were not concerned about his feelings. Judas threw the silver coins into the sanctuary of the temple, and he went away and hung himself. Because it was blood money it was not put into the treasury. Instead, it was used to purchase a tract of land known as the Potter's Field, which was to be used as a cemetery for strangers.

Zechariah 9:9 (cf. Matthew 21:5; Luke 19:32-37)

Rejoice greatly, O Daughter of Zion! Shout, Daughter of Jerusalem! See, your king comes to you, righteous and having salvation, gentle and riding on a donkey.

Jesus' entry into Jerusalem, the heart of Judaism, was understood by the people as a sign of His imminent rule over the Jewish people. They were aware of His miracles, including His power to raise the dead. But little did they know that He was not a political king, whose intention was to stir up a revolution against Roman authority. Jesus was a humble servant sent to offer up His life as a sacrifice for all people, including the Gentiles. This was a reality that the people were unwilling to accept. Verses ten and eleven indicate that Jesus came with a *proclamation of peace and a blood covenant*. As the people cheered Jesus' entry into the city, they could not imagine the events that were to take place.

JESUS' PROPHETIC WORDS

While the prophets predicted the birth, death, and resurrection of the anticipated Messiah, they did not provide a timetable for these life-changing events. It is doubtful that any of them completely understood the type of Messiah that Jesus would be. If so, the Scriptures are silent on this subject. Prophecies tend to be unfolding and do not always translate into clear understanding when they are first echoed or written. It was only after our Lord's resurrection that this became a reality to those searching for truth. Prior to this, the people could not imagine God's Anointed One being a *suffering servant*. The angel told Mary and Joseph that their son would be

Immanuel, meaning *God with us,* and that He would save the people from their sins. (Matthew 1:18-24) But what did all of this mean? They were certainly aware of God's intervention, but they could never have imagined the future events that were destined to change their lives and the world.

During His childhood Jesus had an in-depth understanding of the Scriptures, but we are not provided information about His young adult years. This is probably because His life was no different than other young men at that time. (Luke 2:39-52) When did He realize His divinity and the mission that was set before Him? We know that He had this knowledge when He was baptized by John in the Jordan River, whose ministry He supported. (Matthew 3:13-17; Mark 1:9-11)

After His baptism, Jesus was led by the Holy Spirit into the wilderness for a period of forty days. During this time, He fasted and was relentlessly tempted by Satan. His desert experience, which prepared Him for His suffering and death, was a battle between good and evil. Satan's temptations were aimed at preventing our Lord from going to the cross. But Jesus' obedience to the Father and His knowledge of the Scriptures caused the devil to temporarily withdraw. (Mark 1:12; Luke 4:1-13)

Jesus started preaching the Gospel after John the Baptist was arrested and imprisoned by Herod. He went into Galilee, saying, "The time has come. The kingdom of God is near. Repent, and believe the good news." (Mark 1:14) It was during this time that Jesus began to choose His inner circle of disciples. He often told them about the events that were prophesied, particularly those relating to His death and resurrection. However, they either did not comprehend what He was saying, or they simply refused to accept that He would be tortured and put to death.

Matthew 12:40

For as Jonah was three days and three nights in the belly of a huge fish, so the Son of Man will be three days and three nights in the heart of the earth.

This was Jesus' response to Pharisees and teachers of the law when they wanted to see a miraculous sign from Him to prove His divinity. Jesus told them that no sign would be given to them except the sign of Jonah. It is obvious that they did not understand what He was saying.

Matthew 17:22-23 (Mark 8:31; 9:31; 10:33)

When they came together in Galilee, he said to them, 'The Son of Man is going to be betrayed into the hands of men. They will kill him, and on the third day he will be raised to life.'

In this passage Jesus spoke about His betrayal, arrest and crucifixion. In mentioning His resurrection, He was assuring them that their sadness would turn to joy. While the cross brings sadness, joy and hope are found in our Savior's resurrection.

Matthew 26:1-2

When Jesus had finished saying all these things, he said to his disciples, 'As you know, the Passover is two days away – and the Son of Man will be handed over to be crucified.'

This provides us with a time period when Jesus expected to be crucified. It was told to the disciples to help them prepare for His suffering and death. Needless to say, they were not prepared for the horror that was about to take place.

Matthew 26:24 (Mark 14:21; Luke 22:22)

The Son of Man will go just as it is written about him, but woe to that man who betrays the Son of Man. It would be better for him if he had not been born.

Jesus told His disciples that, although His death was necessary, His betrayer would pay the price. It has been suggested that Judas Iscariot may have escaped eternal damnation, but our Lord's words state otherwise. It is apparent that the remorse Judas experienced did not lead to repentance and faith in Jesus.

Matthew 26:27-28 (Mark 14:22-24; Luke 22:19-20)

Then he took the cup, gave thanks and offered it to them, saying, 'Drink from it, all of you. This is my blood of the covenant, which is poured out for many for the forgiveness of sins.'

Jesus made this statement while eating the Passover meal with His disciples. He used the drink to symbolically represent the blood of God's new covenant with the world. He did the same thing with the Passover bread, stating that it was His body that would be broken for them. These symbols reflect a total life that was given up for humanity. Jesus told His disciples that they should continue this practice as a way of remembering His sacrificial love. Today, most Christians continue this ritual as a form of worship in the sacrament of the Eucharist or Holy Communion. When we prayerfully meditate upon the suffering of Jesus it draws us closer to Him, thus opening up a channel for God's grace. Pondering the crucifixion stirs our emotions and deepens our love for Christ.

Matthew 26:31 (Zechariah 13:7; John 16:32)

Then Jesus said to them, 'This very night you will all fall away on account of me, for it is written: I will strike the shepherd and the sheep of the flock will be scattered.'

These words are rooted in a prophecy given by Zechariah, and they were fulfilled on the day of Jesus' execution. The only disciple present at the crucifixion was John. Fearing reprisals, the other disciples had scattered and took refuge behind closed doors. To be associated with Jesus, even at His crucifixion, was not a chance that they wanted to risk. It was a tense time for our Lord's followers, often resulting in arrest and persecution.

Matthew 26:38-39 (Mark 14:36)

Then he said, 'My soul is overwhelmed with sorrow to the point of death. Stay here and keep watch with me.' Going a little farther, he fell with his face to the ground and prayed. 'My Father, if it is possible, may this cup be taken from me. Yet not as I will, but as you will.'

This is a graphic picture of Jesus' humanity and the suffering that He endured when contemplating His death. The words, *he fell with his face to the ground,* shows the extent of His agony. Jesus wanted His disciples near Him during this time of emotional pain. One can only imagine what they were thinking as they observed their Master.

Mark 8:31-33

He began to teach them that the Son of Man must suffer many things....and that he must be killed and after three days rise again. He spoke plainly about this, and Peter took him aside and began to rebuke him.

Again, it is emphasized that Satan's mission was to prevent Jesus from going to the cross. Although Peter was simply expressing his love for Jesus, our Savior wanted him to understand the schemes and power of the devil. This was a lesson that Peter and the others needed to realize before commencing their ministries.

Mark 10:34 (Luke 18:31-34)

We are going up to Jerusalem, and the Son of Man will be betrayed to the chief priests and teachers of the law. They will condemn him to death and will hand him over to the Gentiles, who will mock and spit on him, flog him and kill him. Three days later he will rise.

In this announcement to His disciples Jesus provides some details of what would occur prior to His execution. He mentioned Jerusalem, as well as specifics relating to the physical abuse that He would endure. According to Luke, the disciples failed to realize what He was saying.

John 1:29

The next day John saw Jesus coming toward him and said, 'Look, the Lamb of God, who takes away the sin of the world.'

John the Baptist knew what Jesus' ultimate sacrifice would be. The words *Lamb of God* were prophetic, meaning that Jesus' sacrifice would replace those required under Mosaic Law. He was both the sin and burnt offering that was lifted up for every generation. Jesus was the *Lamb without blemish,* who came to fulfill the law and Messianic prophecies.

John 2:19

Jesus answered them, 'Destroy this temple, and I will raise it again in three days.'

After Jesus cleared the temple courts of merchants who were disrespecting God's house of prayer, the Jews demanded that He show them a miraculous sign to prove that He had the authority to do such a thing. In response, Jesus prophesied His death and resurrection, referring to His body as a temple. The Jews failed to comprehend what He was saying, believing that He was referring to the Jerusalem temple, which took forty-six years to build. It is clear from this and other scripture passages that Jesus knew how long He would be in the grave.

John 3:16

For God so loved the world that he gave his one and only Son, that whoever believes in him shall not perish but have eternal life.

These words relate to our Lord's conversation with Nicodemus, who had difficulty understanding why God's Anointed One should die for humanity. Jesus made the above statement after illustrating His point by making reference to the bronze snake that Moses lifted up in the wilderness.

John 6:51

I am the living bread that came down from heaven. If anyone eats of this bread, he will live forever. This bread is my flesh, which I will give for the life of the world.

Jesus emphasized that He is the *Bread of Life* that came down from heaven, and those who receive Him will live forever. Like the manna in the desert, Jesus is our life-sustaining food in the wilderness of life. It is His *flesh*, meaning His sacrificial death, which brings life to the world. Some churches understand this within the context of receiving the elements during the Sacrament of Holy Communion.

John 10:11-13

I am the good shepherd. The good shepherd lays down his life for the sheep. No one takes it from me, but I lay it down of my own accord. I have the authority to lay it down and authority to take it up again. This command I received from the Father.

Jesus did not lose His life but rather gave it willingly. Like a *shepherd* protects his flock from predators and, will even lay down his life for them, Jesus laid down His life for us. As the Son of God, He has authority over life and death, a power that has been given to Him by the Father. Throughout the Scriptures we find the analogy of a shepherd being used to express compassionate leadership. Mark records that Jesus considered Himself a shepherd of the people. (Mark 6:34) The writer of Hebrews refers to Jesus as the *Great Shepherd of the Sheep,* and the apostle Peter calls Him the *Chief Shepherd.* (Hebrews 13:20; I Peter 5:4)

John 12:1-8

It was intended that she should save this perfume for the day of my burial....

While visiting the home of Lazarus and his sisters, Martha and Mary, Jesus received a gift that Judas Iscariot thought was wasteful. Mary took a pint of pure nard, an expensive perfume, and she poured it on Jesus' feet and then wiped His feet with her hair. This was significant because, like today, a woman's hair was considered an important part of her beauty. Mary's humility was expressive of her love and respect for Jesus. Judas complained that the perfume could have been sold and the money given to the poor. But rather than being concerned about the poor, Judas was most likely angry and jealous over the attention that Jesus was receiving. Our Lord understood Mary's gift as symbolically relating to the anointing of His body at the time of His burial. After a person died it was customary to wrap the body in cloth and anoint it with perfumes. This was a practice that the Jews learned from the Egyptians.

John 12:23-24

Jesus said, 'The hour has come for the Son of Man to be glorified. I tell you the truth, unless a kernel of wheat falls into the ground and dies, it remains only a single seed. But if it dies, it produces many seeds.'

The death of Jesus has reaped a harvest of forgiven believers who have glorified the Father. Just as a dead seed falling into the ground produces life, the death of Jesus has done the same. Our Savior's crucifixion has opened the door to God's eternal kingdom. The harvest that began at Golgotha continues to this day throughout the world.

John 12:27-28

Now my heart is troubled, and what shall I say? Father, save me from this hour? No, it was for this very reason that I came to this hour. Father, glorify your name.

Although Jesus was feeling the pain of what awaited Him, even seeking to be released from the suffering, He stood firm in His obedience. He knew that He came into the world to give His life as a ransom for our sins.

John 12:31-33

Jesus said, 'Now is the time for judgment on this world; now the prince of this world will be driven out. But I, when I am lifted up from earth, will draw all men to myself.' He said this to show the kind of death that he was going to die.

When Jesus paid the penalty for our sins it was a victory over Satan, the prince of this world. Although evil remains a destructive force, the power of Satan has been destroyed for those who receive Jesus as their Lord and Savior. Although still sinners, we are no longer controlled by the forces of evil. Through the cross our past sins have been erased, and we have become new creatures who live in the power of the Holy Spirit.

John 15:13-15

Greater love has no one than this, that he lay down his life for his friends. You are my friends if you do what I command.

The love that took Jesus to the cross was all inclusive and unconditional. Seldom would a person die for a friend, let alone an enemy. (Romans 5:7) Jesus died for all people, including His enemies. Even during the agony of His crucifixion, He prayed for the forgiveness of His executioners, saying that they did not know what they were doing. The sacrificial love of Christ is the perfect example of forgiveness.

John 18:11

Jesus commanded Peter, 'Put your sword away! Shall I not drink the cup the Father has given me?'

Peter was our Savior's defender, particularly when it came to the thought of Jesus being crucified. His fear, however, later caused him to deny knowing Jesus. After Jesus rose from the dead Peter affirmed his love and faith in Christ, and he became a leader in the Church. In the Garden of Gethsemane Peter tried to forcibly prevent Jesus from being arrested, but he was told to put his sword away. Again, we are told that the crucifixion was the Father's will.

As already mentioned, after Jesus rose from the dead, He accompanied two men who were walking to the village of Emmaus, which was about seven miles from Jerusalem. The men, believing that Jesus was dead, did not immediately recognize Him. They were discussing the events that led to His crucifixion and how the hope of the people died with Him. Jesus interrupted them, saying, "How foolish you are, and how slow of heart to believe all that the prophets have spoken! Did not the Christ have to suffer these things and then enter his glory?" (Luke 24:25-26) The apostle Peter spoke to a group of doubters with similar words, emphasizing that the Hebrew prophets foretold the suffering of Jesus. (Acts 3:17-18)

In his epistles to the churches, Paul always stressed the death of Jesus. His words led them to Golgotha for their forgiveness and reconciliation with God. He told the Christians in Rome that "just as through the disobedience of the one man the many were made sinners, so also through the obedience of the one man many were made righteous." (Romans 5:19) He also emphasized that Christ died for them while they were rebellious and living in sin, thus revealing the depth of God's love. (Romans 5:8) Paul firmly believed that God made Jesus sin for us. He wrote, "God made him who had no sin to be sin for us, so that in him we might become the righteousness of God." (II Corinthians 5:21) Rather than an act of martyrdom, it was God's providence that took Jesus to the cross. This is the central theme of the Scriptures and orthodox Christianity.

There have always been doubters and those who reject the power of the cross. Paul referred to such individuals as enemies of the cross. He said, "For, as I have often told you before and now say again even with tears, many live as enemies of the cross of Christ. Their destiny is destruction, their god is their stomach, and their glory is in their shame. Their mind is on earthly things." (Philippians 3:18-19) In his first letter to the Corinthians, he wrote, "For the message of the cross is foolishness to those who are perishing, but to us who are being saved it is the power of God." (I Corinthians 1:18) The bedrock of Paul's life was in the cross of Jesus Christ. He said that he would never boast except in the cross of his Savior. (Galatians 6:14)

Like Paul, the apostle Peter also taught that Jesus bore our sins in His body. (I Peter 2:24-25) Although we cannot comprehend the theological depth of this truth, it reinforces both the purpose and results of Jesus' sacrifice. Peter also stressed the finality of Jesus' sacrifice when he wrote, "Christ died for sins once for all, the righteous for the unrighteous, to bring you God. He was put to death in the body but made alive by the Spirit." (I Peter 3:18) It was necessary for Israel's high priests to continuously offer up sacrifices on behalf of the people, but Jesus Christ is the one sacrifice accepted by God for all generations. His obedience brought an end to the sacrificial system. (Philemon 2:8; Hebrews 7:27-28; 9:11-14) In Christ we have an intercessor who speaks to the Father on our behalf.

The first-century Jewish historian Flavius Josephus (37-100 A.D.) referenced the death and resurrection of Jesus Christ in his writings. What follows is a paraphrase of the original writing:

> There was about this time a wise man named Jesus – if it is lawful to call him a man, for he was a doer of wonderful works – a teacher of the type of men who enjoy hearing the truth. He drew many of the Jews and Gentiles to him; he was the Christ. When Pilate, at the suggestion of the Jewish leaders, condemned him to the cross, those who loved him at first did not forsake him, for he appeared to them alive the third day, as the divine prophets had foretold, along with many other wonderful things concerning him. The tribe of Christians named for him still exists today. (Josephus: *Thrones of Blood*, 61)

DIMENSIONS OF THE CROSS

Humanity had lost its way, but there was a plan of redemption in place that brought the Son of God into our midst. The apostle John wrote, "The Word became flesh and lived for a while among us. We have seen his glory, the glory of the one and only Son, who came from the Father, full of grace and truth." (John 1:14) The humanity of Jesus enabled Him to completely identify with the human condition. In my book *Ministry to the Incarcerated* are the following words:

> Jesus entered the company of the despised, the tortured and the rejected. His public execution with two robbers can be interpreted as a sign of solidarity with these lost people. As the community of the crucified Jesus, we are drawn into his self-surrender, into his solidarity with the lost, and into his public suffering. His suffering is in this respect not exclusive but inclusive and leads to compassion.

What follows are the spiritual dimensions that we find in our Lord's sacrificial death:

Fulfillment of Mosaic Law

The Hebrew sacrifices that were to atone for sin have their fulfillment in Jesus Christ. While the law exposed sin, it lacked the power to change one's heart toward God. It is through the sacrificial love of Christ and the power of the Holy Spirit that people are changed.

Substitution

The Scriptures emphasize that Jesus died in our place, the righteous for the unrighteous. What our Savior accomplished was impossible for us. It was the Lord who initiated our salvation, providing the path for reconciliation and redemption.

God's Love

Prior to the cross, humanity realized the power, justice, and the holiness of God, but they failed to recognize His unconditional and universal love. It is the death of Jesus that takes us into the heart of God. The cross tells us that there is no limit to God's love.

Justification

To justify means to be declared righteous before God. It relates to forgiveness and our release from divine judgment. Rather than our good deeds, it is our faith in the atoning sacrifice of Jesus that declares us righteous before God.

Propitiation

God's satisfaction with the intercession of His Son has removed His anger toward our sins. It is this satisfaction that opens the channel for us to receive His grace.

Example of a Servant

Our Lord's death is the ultimate example of being God's servant. Jesus once asked His disciples if the servant is greater than the master. When Jesus offered up His life, He showed us what it means to be humble and obedient to God. There is no higher calling than to lay down your life for others; to give your life for a higher purpose.

Adoption

It is our new life in Christ, made possible through the cross, which makes us God's adopted children. As God's children we share in the blessings of His eternal kingdom. These blessings begin now and will have their fulfillment when Jesus returns.

Sanctification

The adoption that comes through Christ sets us apart for God's work. Although we remain in this world, we are spiritually separated from it. This separation enables us to be witnesses of truth and grace.

Power Over Temptation

Beginning in the wilderness, Jesus stood firm upon God's Word. He overcame every temptation known to humanity. We must also confront temptation through our faith in God's Word and the power of the cross.

Judgment of the Sinful Nature

Although we remain sinners, the sacrifice of Jesus has broken the power of sin over our lives. Sin no longer controls us.

Resurrection

Beyond the suffering of the cross was the resurrection. When Jesus rose from the dead His mission on earth was finished, and our salvation was sealed. Within the cross lay our resurrection power and the hope of eternal life. Without the cross there would be no resurrection.

Jesus wants us to remember the love that led Him to the cross. He knew that after His ascension, few people beyond His inner circle, would take the time to contemplate and internalize His suffering and death. When sharing the Passover meal with His disciples He provided a graphic means by which His sacrifice should be remembered. He emphasized the importance of this act, and He commanded His disciples to continue the ritual. The suffering and death of Jesus speaks to His identity with sinners, thus enabling His compassion and power to enter our lives.

The Eucharist can be understood in the following ways:

- When we prayerfully receive the sacrament, we are internalizing the living and transforming spirit of Christ, which includes His compassion and sacrificial love.

- As a memorial, the elements of the wine and bread serve as a penetrating reminder that Jesus literally shed His blood and gave His body for our salvation. Reflection upon this draws us closer to Him.

- The Eucharist emphasizes Christian unity. There is one body, one Spirit and one Church. This bond speaks to the barriers that cause divisions.

- We realize that the Church is a mystical body that is brought together and empowered by the Holy Spirit. Rather than a secular organization, it is a spiritual building that is molded by God through the faith and love of people.

- The sacrament confronts our own suffering, reminding us that in Jesus Christ there is victory. It also makes us realize that God is in the midst of our suffering and that it serves a higher purpose. This is a truth that the apostle Paul lived and taught.

- When meditating upon the cross we experience a sorrow that leads us to confession.

- Holy Communion fills us with thanksgiving and praise for the gift of Jesus Christ.

What was foretold by the prophets became a reality that would forever change the world. The Messiah, who had the power to forgive sins, heal the sick and raise the dead, came back to life after being tortured and crucified. All doubts were now put to rest, for Jesus truly is the Son of God. He appeared to His disciples and many other people during a period of forty days prior to His ascension. They saw Him in the flesh, witnessed His wounds of crucifixion, and they listened to His teachings about the kingdom of God and the promise of His return. Everything that Jesus previously told them came true, and they were overjoyed and filled with hope. Just before His ascension He gathered His disciples together and commissioned them to preach the Gospel and to baptize believers. Since that day the Gospel of Jesus Christ has been preached throughout the world, transforming the lives of those who live in faith.

The humanity and scars of Jesus will forever be part of the Godhead and infused into our lives. There is nothing in all creation that can separate us from the love of God that is found in Jesus Christ. There is no greater message given to humanity.

—CHAPTER THREE—

Christian Life and Ministry

PULPIT MESSAGES

The art of preaching is difficult to define, for it is unlike any other form of verbal communication. In some respects, it is a bugle call that alerts us to our spiritual complacency and sin, while at the same time challenging us to grow in the image of Christ. This, of course, speaks to our service to God and one another. Sermons must reach a diverse group of people, and this needs to be considered when preparing the message. While sermons need to emphasize God's love and forgiveness, they should never dilute the reality and destructiveness of sin. It is only by confronting the sin in our lives that we are able to experience spiritual cleansing and renewal.

Messages that address our deepest needs must be biblical, realistic and practical. Christians are not removed from the world, which is a truth that our Savior stressed with His apostles. Jesus told them, "In the world you will have troubles. But take heart! I have overcome the world." (John 16:33) To suggest that our faith will somehow remove us from trials is not biblical. The question is not whether the trials will come, but rather when they will occur and how long they will last. We were never promised a trouble-free life, but God does provide the grace that will sustain us. In fact, when the Lord is in our life our trials make us stronger. The apostle Paul said that in Jesus Christ we become more than conquerors, meaning that we grow through tribulation and are better prepared to help others. There is a tendency for people to believe that their Christianity will somehow keep them from the afflictions that face other people. Sermons claiming that one's faith will remove them from life's struggles are detrimental to a person's understanding of God's grace and promises.

Disease, personal loss and death, are part of this life, and no one is excluded from these painful situations. Pastors are given the responsibility of preparing people for these trying times. This can be communicated by studying the lives of the apostles and countless Christians who have suffered throughout history. Actually, some Christians suffer in this life because of their faith and the work that they do in Jesus' name. The apostles were in Jesus' inner circle, yet they suffered persecution and ultimately became martyrs for their faith.

It is important that clergy emphasize the brevity of life, and the fact that our earthly journey involves challenges and pain. Christians serve God in a world that has been tainted by sin, and the influences and trials are real. Rather than provide superficial, simplistic, and patent responses for the difficulties of life, the Church must be honest with God's people by conveying messages that are realistic. It is a wonderful feeling to engage in animate and joyful worship, but the realities of life must be addressed by the Church. The objective of ministry is to help people develop a depth of understanding and faith that will enable them to become more than conquerors. This is where inner peace and true joy is found.

Many pastors desire some flexibility when preaching, which allows them the opportunity to insert thoughts that were not part of their preparation. This approach permits the movement of the Holy Spirit during the time of delivery. But pastors are not excused from necessary sermon preparation. Sermons need a structure that educates and provides the insights that awaken and challenge the listener. Without these elements there is a lack of power, as well as a tendency to be redundant and shallow. When this occurs, parishioners become confused and lose interest. Once you have listened to an educated and gifted pastor who is well prepared, it is disheartening to be at the receiving end of an unskilled communicator who lacks knowledge and preparation. Being a pastor is an awesome responsibility, and it is unfortunate that some clergy do not realize this. It is a sin to violate the trust that God has placed in His servants, especially when it comes to communicating God's Word.

People attend worship services because they have questions and needs that only the Lord can address. They are aware of a void in their life, and they turn to God for answers. They expect the Lord to speak to them through their pastor, who will hopefully provide the knowledge, encouragement, and hope, that will help guide them. The Church is God's instrument to show us the path to spiritual formation and service, and the Sunday morning message has a key part in this. Without well-prepared sermons that speak to our hearts, we leave Sunday morning worship without the spiritual food that we desire and desperately need. Clergy who become complacent in their preaching ministries are failing the Lord and the people in their care.

CHRISTIAN EDUCATION
Children's Ministry

In one of my parishes there were only six children, but we established Sunday school classes for them. This was possible because of committed parents who were willing to give their time and talents to make this happen. Sometimes there were only a few children in church, but an effort was made to meet the needs of those in attendance with material that was appropriate to their age. But a problem does exist when there is a considerable age difference between children in a small class. To confront this, we had individuals who were on standby to assist. This may seem extreme when we are only talking about a small number of children, but every child must have the opportunity to learn about the Lord. A child's spiritual education should start at the earliest possible age, and the Church is called to do its part. Some leaders believe that there should be a certain number of children before starting a class. This belief not only delays the education of some children, but without a program in place visitors with children will be discouraged from returning. I am not implying that parents should depend upon the Church for their child's spiritual life, for nothing can replace the education and Christian example of parents.

The apostles once rebuked parents who were bringing their children to Jesus for a blessing. They probably believed that the children were an annoyance and wasting Jesus' time. When Jesus saw this, He became indignant and said, "Let the little children come to me, and do not hinder them, for the kingdom of God belongs to such as these. I tell you the truth, anyone who will not receive the kingdom of God like a little child will never enter it." After saying this, Jesus took the children in His arms and blessed them. (Mark 10:13-16) This is a clear picture of our Savior's love for children, as well as the responsibility that He has placed upon the Church to protect and guide them.

On another occasion, Jesus used the humility of children as an example of discipleship. He called a little child and had him stand among the apostles, saying, "I tell you the truth, unless you change and become like little children, you will never enter the kingdom of heaven." He also told them that whoever welcomes a child in His name also welcomes Him. In addition, Jesus let them know that there will be severe consequences for anyone who leads a child to sin. (Matthew 18:1-7) The Church sometimes dismisses the needs of children, but Jesus sternly reminds us of our continuing responsibility. We are called to pray for our children and to help provide the nurturing that they require. This includes our support for parents, asking the Lord to give them the love, wisdom and patience, to be examples of holiness. Sometimes it does take a village to keep our children on the righteous path. The more positive influences they have, the better their chance of establishing the Christian roots that will endure through life's changes and challenges.

Teenage Ministries

Teen ministries require patient and creative leaders who are knowledgeable in the Scriptures, as well as the peer pressures and transitional concerns of young people. Teenagers experience rapid changes in their lives, and their emotions are often in turmoil. They live under parental authority, while at the same time desiring their independence. Although these dynamics are normal, they often result in family conflict and anger. Many young people are in a fragile state, and their life can go into a tailspin over minor situations. Their life is constantly in flux, which makes it difficult for them to experience a sense of security and well-being. They also see the struggles of their parents, and this often adds to their anxiety and uncertainty about the future. The thought of going to college presents a host of concerns, including finances and the discipline that a college education requires. Even though a career and marriage may be far in the future, there is often anxiety relating to these transitional events. With many of these concerns there is an underlying fear of failure.

The Church has an important role in helping young people find structure, boundaries, and the spiritual life that will carry them into the future. Christian education can establish self-worth, bring meaning to life, and help teens realize their potential in Jesus Christ. This is accomplished by focusing upon God's unconditional love and the strength that is found in Christ. Our value before God is found in the sacrificial love of Jesus. It has nothing to do with appearance, popularity, school grades or accomplishments. The ministry of Jesus teaches us about God's boundless love for all people. Through biblical teachings, teenagers also learn about forgiveness, respect, reconciliation, and a disciplined lifestyle that brings glory to God. While these lessons are for everyone, it is important that they are learned at a young age. Parents are cognizant of the negative influences that plague their children; therefore, they can be an asset to teen ministries. A church may have a youth pastor or adults who are gifted working with teens, but parents should always play a role in their child's Christian education. They have hands-on experiences and the maturity that makes them indispensable participants.

Most teen ministries include a variety of activities that are aimed at forging relational bonds with their peers and the adult members of the congregation. While these fellowships are important for social development, they should also have a spiritual dimension that helps build Christian understanding and character. When considering the uncertainty of life and how quickly time passes, the Church must take advantage of every opportunity to help our young people with their spiritual development. The seeds that are sown during these years may not immediately germinate, but what chance do teenagers have if the seeds are not sown? Whether we plow the ground, sow the seeds, water the field or reap the harvest, we must share in our Savior's grace to our young people.

Adult Education

Depending upon one's perception of the Church and their personal journey, adult education presents important questions. In other words, what subjects are most important for spiritual growth? Should published materials be the norm for all Christian education? What are the topics that parishioners believe will help them in their daily lives? Should we give equal time to both the Hebrew Scriptures and the New Testament? These are just a few of the questions that pastors and congregational leaders need to consider. Obviously, the more we think about Christian education, the more questions we have. We should also give consideration to personal factors, such as age, traditions, educational levels, and the religious backgrounds of parishioners. This information provides insight into how some individuals may think about certain topics. For example, while politics should be avoided, political beliefs and concerns sometimes surface and influence class discussions. This is a dangerous area for pastors and teachers, primarily because it can lead to relational conflict and division.

When reflecting upon adult education my first thought relates to the teachers. It is essential that all teachers be mature Christians who are committed to Christ and the ministry of the Church. Interviews with the pastor and the education committee can determine where a person is in their spiritual life. Having taught in both university and church settings, I know how difficult and challenging the classroom can be. Everyone is at a different place in life, carrying baggage from the past, as well as having present issues to work through. When considering the dynamics in a diverse educational environment, obtaining the best qualified teacher is obviously important. This can be a difficult task, but with prayer, time and patience, it can become a reality.

On a home visit to an elderly man who sometimes visited my last parish, I found myself in disbelief when he shared his religious life with me. He was a well-groomed and educated gentleman who lived alone since the death of his wife. I found him to be soft spoken, polite, and very attentive during our conversation. As we interacted, he informed me of his past church leadership positions, which included teaching an adult Sunday school class. But what followed was a shock! He told me that it was impossible for him to believe in the teachings of Jesus Christ. As a professional scientist, he thought that the Gospels offer false comfort and hope. As I listened to him, I could not believe what I was hearing, especially knowing that for years he taught an adult class in a large church.

Rather than debate theology, the Lord led me to share my life with him, specifically how I came to know Jesus Christ as my Lord and Savior. He listened intently to my story, but there was no indication that his heart was responding. Before leaving his residence, I suggested that he pray about his lack of understanding and disbelief. I also told him that I would keep him in my prayers. Two months after my visit he died, and I was asked by his son to officiate at his funeral. Needless to say, it was difficult to know how to communicate as I alluded to his life. I decided to spend most of the service speaking to the living about the hope that is in our Savior.

This may have been an unusual and extreme case, but it alerts us to a reality in the Church. There are individuals who are leading groups without having a personal relationship with Jesus Christ. It also reveals the responsibility that pastors have in choosing spiritual and knowledgeable individuals for teaching positions. While problems can develop with mature Christian teachers, the wrong person can be devastating to a church. Relieving an unqualified teacher is painful for everyone, especially if the teacher is an admired member of the congregation.

As I previously emphasized, we are a New Testament Church living in the grace of Jesus Christ, which should tell us something about educational priorities. To study the Hebrew Scriptures with their revelations, prophecies, lessons for life, and how certain writings relate to Jesus, is important for one's overall understanding. But it is the teachings of Jesus and the apostles that must be our primary focus. In Jesus Christ we find answers to perplexing questions, the strength to face life's trials, and the light that offers eternal hope. There is a power in the words of Jesus and the apostles that cannot be found in other areas of the Scriptures. Matthew tells us that Jesus' teachings amazed the people, for He taught as one who had the authority of God. (Matthew 7:28-29) While the entire Bible is inspired by God and valuable for our spiritual journey, it is the teachings of Christ and His apostles that bring understanding and spiritual renewal.

Rather than always using published Sunday school materials that have limited benefits, it is important that skilled and knowledgeable teachers develop some lessons that speak to particular concerns that people have. I have learned that many Christians lack basic understandings, and they have questions on a variety of subjects that published materials do not explore. These publications are sometimes mundane and superficial, lacking the depth that challenge thought and dialogue. It may take energy and time to create meaningful teaching outlines, but the results are rewarding for everyone. Christians need lessons that open their minds to the mysteries of God, while at the same time speaking to them in a realistic and practical way. Church leaders need to know that education is the key to objective thinking and a channel to strengthen one's faith and commitment to Jesus Christ and His Church.

Special Classes

In addition to weekly church ministries, there is a need for specialized classes. While some of these opportunities may only be given at certain times, others should be available as needs arise. For instance, membership classes are only offered when individuals are preparing to join a church. These classes are normally taught by the pastor, who sets the format and the number of weeks that the class will meet. People who transfer their membership from one congregation to another within the same denomination may not be required to attend such classes. I believe that this is a mistake, for these classes provide a review of doctrine and enable new members to ask the pastor questions. They also acquaint people with the uniqueness of the congregation that they are joining.

In some congregations the children of new members are also given an indoctrination to help them feel welcome. This is normally an informal situation that is led by an adult member, with young people participating. It is difficult attending a new church; therefore, all family members need to feel comfortable with the transition. The early months will unquestionably determine the success of the affiliation and whether the family will remain at the church and participate in its ministry. We tend to welcome people when they first attend church services, but they are often forgotten along the way.

Confirmation classes are another type of specialized education, intended to prepare young people for church membership and a lifetime commitment to Jesus Christ. The appropriate age for these studies is a difficult decision for pastors, particularly when parents want their child to begin at a certain time. I have taught teenagers who were unable to comprehend basic doctrines, learn biblical history, and understand important scripture. At the conclusion of these courses, which may last two years, confirmation graduates stand before God and the local church to make a profession of faith that brings them into church membership.

The subject matter in confirmation classes is too difficult for most children. In fact, I am certain that many adults would find these courses challenging. As such, I question the entire confirmation process, including the expectations that are held. I am not suggesting that we abandon the concept, but we need to find a better way to provide our children with the essentials of Christianity. Realizing the learning limitations of children, we need to create programs that are less demanding and more enjoyable. Eliminating some of the religious rhetoric and details relating to Church history would be a good starting point. In preparing this section, I reviewed the denominational material that I have used, and I am convinced that we must develop a less painful way to bring understanding to our children.

Being a pastor has taught me that many parishioners do not know the basic tenets of Christianity. While this is difficult to understand, complacency and the absence of spiritual discipline are contributing factors. People may attend worship services on a regular basis, but they give little thought to studying the Scriptures and engaging in a devotional life that will impact upon their lives, enabling spiritual maturity.

The writer of Hebrews exhorted early Christians to move on to maturity. He told them that at a certain point they should be teachers of their faith, instead of always needing to be taught by others. He urged them to partake of solid food, rather than remaining on milk. (Hebrews 5:12) The Scriptures repeatedly tell us to progress beyond the fundamentals to a life of maturity and holiness. Just as poorly-built houses cannot withstand the storms of life, our failure to build a strong spiritual structure will bring the same results. In every area of life we want the best for ourselves, but when it comes to our spiritual life we settle for much less.

Other important areas of education include topics relating to Lent, personal loss, and marriage and family issues. In addition, some churches provide classes for individuals with serious illnesses and those going through difficult transitions. These ministries are employed according to the needs of a congregation. Some churches utilize volunteer professionals for certain studies, which is an approach that maximizes the effectiveness of a ministry. In some situations, two or more congregations may combine as a way to meet a desired attendance.

Special studies during Lent bring us into a renewed understanding of God's love. The weeks leading up to the crucifixion of Jesus should be a time of deep reflection. During Lent we are confronted with Jesus' suffering and the purpose of His death. The suffering that Jesus endured is beyond our comprehension, for it not only included physical and emotional pain but also His separation from the Father at the time of His death. This is the love that God has for every sinner, and it is during Lent that we must experience it in penetrating ways. As we meditate upon the atoning sacrifice of our Lord, our hearts are stirred with gratitude and a deep sense of humility. This response revives our spirit and brings us closer to God. The personal reflections and graphic teachings during this holy season should have lasting effects upon us.

Those who prayerfully reflect upon the death of Jesus become recipients of special gifts, including God's restorative peace.

Paul describes it as a peace that transcends all understanding and one that will keep our hearts and minds in Jesus Christ. (Philippians 4:7) God's peace is received when we honestly open our hearts, allowing the cleansing power of the Holy Spirit to wash away our sins and negative attitudes. It is a peace that restores our humanity, enabling us to love all people. To harbor anything against another person is to live with inner conflict. The peace of God is a spiritual gift that removes the animosity and bitterness that destroys the soul. We live in a world that lacks personal and interpersonal peace, which is the reason why we are overwhelmed with violence. Lent reminds us of the sins that prevent us from receiving and sharing the peace of Christ.

When Jesus was experiencing the excruciating agony of crucifixion, He made seven brief statements. They were brief because of His pain and the difficulty that He had breathing. Time should be set aside during Lent to reflect upon these words of love and power. The following statements are also known as the Seven Words:

1. Father, forgive them, for they do not know what they are doing.

Jesus asked the Father to forgive those who tortured Him and were waiting for His death. While others would feel hatred and a desire for retribution, Jesus wanted the Father to completely forgive the cruelty of His enemies.

2. Today, you will be with me in Paradise.

These words were said to a criminal who was crucified next to Jesus. The condemned man asked Jesus to remember him when He entered His kingdom. Jesus responded by telling him that he would be in Paradise that very day. Again, we see our Savior's forgiving heart and His promise of salvation for those who have faith in Him.

3. Woman, behold your son. John, behold your mother.

Rather than focusing upon His own suffering and death, Jesus was concerned about the needs of others. He wanted His mother and the apostle John to be supportive of one another, knowing that the future was going to be difficult.

4. My God, my God, why have you forsaken me?

This agonizing cry reveals the depth of Jesus' suffering. Some scholars believe that He may not have known that the Father would leave Him to die alone. But this is the sinner's death, and it was the Father's will for His Son.

5. I thirst.

Jesus shared in our humanity, having the same physical needs. These words reveal our Lord's extreme dehydration.

6. It is finished.

Jesus obeyed the Father's will to the very end. His entire life was a sacrificial offering for humanity. He gave His life and could do no more.

7. Father, into your hands I commend my spirit.

Jesus not only offered up His life for us, but He also sacrificed His life for the Father, trusting Him in the midst of His suffering and death.

Although brief, these statements show us what it means to have faith in the midst of suffering. We also see a love and forgiveness that forces us to examine ourselves. This is the message of Lent. As we ponder the sacrifice of Christ, may each of us seek His faith, obedience, love, and forgiving heart.

Small Study Groups

Bible study groups that meet in private residences have been increasing in many communities. They are normally comprised of people who desire to study the Scriptures in a relaxed and social environment, as opposed to the more structured setting of a church. Although the classes are often started by individuals who attend the same church, they sometimes have an open attendance policy. These participants are serious about their faith and spiritual development, often having the desire to study material that may not be offered in a local church. The informal setting allows for more dialogue and personal sharing, thereby creating a sense of well-being and mutual support.

Along with the benefits of these gatherings, there are certain problems that may develop. Within any group of people there are individuals who become the recognized leaders and authority figures, and Bible studies are no exception. This can lead to competitive personalities and control issues that cause interpersonal stress. Similar situations also occur in church settings, but they are less pronounced due to the disciplined nature of the class and the accepted recognition of a leader who guides the discussions. When certain individuals control and monopolize discussions, others may withdraw or even stop attending. While this may not be the norm, it is something to consider when forming these groups.

There are other issues that these study groups encounter, one of which relates to the teachers. Some people feel inadequate leading a Bible study, which may place a burden on others who attend. These situations can change as mutual encouragement increases, bringing confidence to those who are uncomfortable in teaching roles. However, depending upon the personalities of the people, it is also possible for personal inadequacies to be reinforced. As these groups continue to meet, other dynamics may surface. For instance, as people become comfortable with one another personal issues are sometimes shared. I have seen Bible studies digress into very sensitive areas of discussion that cast a shadow over the group.

COMMUNAL PRAYER

Christians know the necessity of having a personal prayer life, but little thought is given to praying together as a congregation. In most churches the only time parishioners pray together is during the worship service, and it is normally a brief confession or invocation that is read in unison. If we believe that prayer is important in our personal lives, how can we think otherwise when it comes to the life of the Church? It is impossible for congregations to know the Lord's will if they do not pray for guidance. In all my years of ministry I have only heard a few church leaders suggest communal prayer for God's leading. While corporate prayer is practiced in some denominations and faith groups, it is not the norm for many Christian congregations.

The apostles knew that the Lord's work could not be accomplished without communal prayer. After Jesus' ascension they immediately met together for prayer, seeking the Lord's grace and direction for both their personal lives and the life of the Church. (Acts 1:12-14) The apostles prayed for wisdom and the power to proclaim the Gospel. They also sought the faith and strength that would enable them to stand firm when confronted with resistance and persecution. Questions about leadership and mission were always a matter for prayer, as they knew that it is God who chooses leaders and sends out workers according to His plans. When the apostles needed to replace Judas, they prayed together for the Lord's leading. According to Luke, the apostles proposed two men, Joseph called Barsabbas and Matthias. They prayed to God, saying, "Lord, you know everyone's heart. Show us which of these two you have chosen to take over the apostolic ministry, which Judas left to go where he belongs." Then they cast lots, and the lot fell to Matthias, who was added to the eleven apostles. (Acts 1:23-26)

For a congregation to move in any direction without gathering together for prayer is to assume that human wisdom is superior to that of our Creator. Without communal prayer we fall into secularism, becoming a worldly institution whose decisions are made by a few people. When church leaders make decisions without the entire congregation gathering for divine guidance, the assumption is that only the leaders know God's will. This makes church members feel isolated and unimportant to the ministry. When a church prays together about important matters the people are more inclined to accept the decision of the majority. There will always be those who disagree, but at least they will know that the outcome resulted from prayer. Without this process we leave God out of our decisions and exclude the people who are needed to support the ministry.

Congregations that pray together are expressing humility and their faith in God, as well as showing respect for each other. They recognize the Lord's authority over the Church and their lives, while at the same time creating a bond of mutual trust with one another that improves relationships. In addition, parishioners are providing an example for their children. As young people begin to participate in congregational prayer, they will realize God's grace and power in decision making. We forget that this is an important example for the youth in our churches. When we practice communal prayer, we open up a channel of grace for both present and future generations.

UNITY IN THE CHURCH

It was during my tenure as a state prison chaplain that I was reminded of the need for unity among Christians. My inmate congregation was one of extreme diversity, and there were always spiritual debates among the men that sometimes led to conflict. This prompted me to teach a midweek study on the necessity of Christian unity. My preparation included the development of an exhaustive biblical outline with pertinent scripture. References that speak to God's command for unity are found throughout the Scriptures, both in the Hebrew Bible and the

New Testament. The ultimate example of unity is found within the Godhead between Father, Son, and Holy Spirit.

Saint Paul addressed the need for Christian unity in his epistles to the churches that he and his co-workers established. In his first letter to the Corinthians, he wrote, "I appeal to you, brothers, in the name of our Lord Jesus Christ, that all of you agree with one another so that there may be no divisions among you and that you may be perfectly united in mind and thought." (I Corinthians 1:10) In this same letter, Paul mentioned the jealousy and quarreling among the people, telling them that they were still worldly. He saw that the foundations he had established were being torn apart by sin. (I Corinthians 3) The apostle James also alluded to division when he spoke about the destructive power of the tongue. He said, "The tongue is a small part of the body, but it makes great boasts." (James 3:5-6)

The call for unity among God's people was heard long before the time of Christ and the apostles. In Psalm 133 King David wrote, "How good and pleasant it is when brothers live together in unity! It is like precious oil poured on the head, running down on the beard, running down on Aaron's beard, down upon the collar of his robes. It is as if the dew of Hermon were falling on Mount Zion. For there the Lord bestows his blessing." These words communicate the peace and serenity that interpersonal unity brings. Obviously, those who acquire this peace should make every effort to maintain it through prayer and meditation.

Without relational unity the Church is no different than a secular organization, but this truth is seldom emphasized in our local ministries. Pastors and teachers may offer brief references to Christian unity, but there are seldom biblical teachings on this important subject. Different beliefs exist between Christian denominations and within every congregation. Some of these differences have led to pride and superior attitudes that not only destroy unity, but also communicate a poor witness. Jesus left His throne of glory to unite with humanity and to give His love to all people. The question is, what are we willing to give in order to unite people in His love? Is the servant any greater than the Master? Jesus commands that we be peacemakers who bring people together. (Matthew 5:9) He prayed for all believers when He said:

> My prayer is not only for the apostles. I pray for those who will believe in me through their message, that all of them may be one, Father, just as you are in me and I am in you. May they also be in us so that the world may believe that you sent me. I have given them the glory that you gave me, that they may be one as we are one: I in them and you in me. May they be brought to complete unity to let the world know that you sent me and have loved them even as you have loved me. (John 17:20-23)

Years ago, I read *The Life of Mahatma Gandhi* by Louis Fischer. This book gives penetrating insights into relational harmony in the midst of strife and violence. Gandhi sacrificed his life bringing people together in a bond of peace and unity. He believed in human nature and in the importance of every person.

Being aware of his own defects, he accepted others as they were. Because his friends knew that he would always forgive them, they were not afraid to share their thoughts and feelings with him. Although he was not a Christian, Gandhi lived the teachings of Jesus. In fact, he always kept a copy of our Savior's *Beatitudes* with him. Gandhi could not understand why Christians did not exemplify the teachings of Christ, which is a question that we must ask ourselves. How can we claim to be disciples of Jesus if we disregard His teachings on love, forgiveness, and Christian unity? We will not be perfect in this life, but we can possess a pure heart that communicates a peaceful spirit of unity.

Paul told Christians that, although they were many members, they formed one body in Jesus Christ. He urged them to do everything possible for the needy and to consider others better than themselves. (Romans 12:1-21) He wrote, "May the God who gives endurance and encouragement give you a spirit of unity among yourselves as you follow Christ Jesus, so that with one heart and mouth you may glorify the God and Father of our Lord Jesus Christ." (Romans 15:5-6) Paul's letters to Christians stressed the need to be united in mind and spirit. He knew that regardless of differences, every believer is baptized by the same Spirit, and they should strive to be at peace with one another. To the Galatians he said, "As we have opportunity, let us do good to all people, especially those who belong to the family of believers." (Galatians 6:10) Paul linked Christian unity back to Abraham's seed, when he wrote, "There is neither Jew nor Greek, slave or free, male or female, for you are all one in Christ Jesus. If you belong to Christ, then you are Abraham's seed, and heirs according to the promise." (Galatians 3:28-29) The Ephesians also received Paul's admonition regarding the need to be united in Christ. These are his words to the Christians in Ephesus:

> Be completely humble and gentle; be patient, bearing with one another in love. Make every effort to keep the unity of the Spirit through the bond of peace. There is one body and one Spirit – just as you were called to one hope when you were called – one Lord, one faith, one baptism; one God and Father of all, who is over all and through all and in all. (Ephesians 4:2-6)

Paul reminds us that unity is God's command for the universal Church, which means that we must assume the humility and sacrificial love of Christ. Rather than allowing divisiveness to develop, Christians must rejoice and celebrate their forgiveness and salvation in Jesus Christ. When Christians argue over their differences, the bond that unites them is lost. On the Day of Judgment, everyone will have their theology corrected. We will also be told of the times when we failed to love others. When religious groups assume superior attitudes, they become guilty of unrighteous judgments. Rather than always looking at other individuals and churches, the Lord wants us to continuously examine ourselves. This in itself will help bring a spirit of unity within the Church.

COMMUNITY OUTREACH AND GROWTH

Churches are always concerned about attendance and membership numbers, primarily because it relates to their survival and understanding of successful ministry. While some congregations are growing, many of them struggle just to maintain the status quo. Pastors who are in these churches feel continuing pressure as they try to revive their ministries. Church growth is both difficult and complex because it involves multiple factors. Today's families are constantly on the move with activities and working long hours, and this situation will not change. There are also economic issues that relate to congregational involvement and growth. When economic conditions are poor, families struggle to support local ministries. This is especially true when churches are on the verge of financial collapse. It is not unusual for families to leave ministries that are always asking for money.

In addition to the obvious deterrents to church growth, there are often latent factors. Some congregations suffer from stigmas that have existed for years. They may result from internal problems, the conservative nature of the congregation, or the lack of a viable ministry. Sometimes, it is simply the condition of the church. Church buildings that are not properly maintained communicate a negative message to a community. When people do not care about their place of worship, observers tend to make judgments about the ministry. We find this same truth in residential areas where people do not take proper care of their homes.

Control issues within a congregation can present serious problems. It is not unusual for churches to be influenced by individuals and families that have a long history in the congregation and community. The situations are magnified when they are large financial contributors. It is common for pastors to leave these congregations prematurely, which leads to more difficulties for the church. Congregations that cannot keep a pastor frequently experience divisions and loss of membership. Interim clergy assume these vacancies until another pastor is installed, which may be months or even years. These changes are unsettling and bring a sense of insecurity among the people. I am aware of churches that have continuously gone through this cycle, reaching a point when they could no longer support a pastor.

Small parishes with more than one church are particularly difficult to transform. Because of their size and a pastor's limited time with each congregation, these churches tend to be maintenance ministries that do not grow. With some parishes, it is a challenge to just keep the doors open. Those who pastor multiple parishes experience emotional and physical exhaustion as they try to address the traditions and concerns of each congregation. For obvious reasons, new members are seldom drawn to these ministries. The absence of young families and educational programs cause visitors to look elsewhere. Additionally, many of these churches are in sparsely-populated areas, and this limits the number of people who may be interested in attending.

Trying to revive small churches in rural areas is sometimes impossible, which is a truth that is reinforced after continuous efforts by different pastors. The problem is convincing church members of this reality. Parishioners have a difficult time letting go of a fellowship and church building that has been part of their family history. Also, the thought of terminating a ministry translates into a failure and betrayal that some people will not accept. After all, this is God's house that is being closed. These strong feelings are understandable, but when a congregation has dwindled to a few families after continuous efforts to increase membership, a decision must be made.

I assisted at a multiple charge parish where the attendance in each of three congregations was less than twenty people. Can you imagine the toll that this takes on a pastor over a long period of time? If small congregations were to consolidate there may be a chance for church growth. The increased number of people would add ministry opportunities and make the church more inviting to new families. Unfortunately, few multiple charge parishes are willing to take this step. They would rather continue struggling, hoping that a miracle will occur through the employment of the next pastor. The difficulties and stress in these parishes often results in a negativity that cannot be reversed.

Another barrier to community outreach is secularism. We live in a materialistic society that affects our philosophy of life, including our understanding of the Church. Unless people need a particular service, such as baptism, confirmation, weddings or funerals, they are not drawn to Christian ministry. In fact, some people only view the Church as a service provider, rather than a place of fellowship, worship, and spiritual formation. This mentality is only resolved when people realize their spiritual needs. Churches that have strong preaching and educational ministries are obviously better prepared to confront this situation.

Lay leadership may also influence church outreach and growth. Pastors depend upon congregational leaders to perform certain tasks, but the negative attitudes and inactivity of some leaders is detrimental to ministry. Individuals who assume leadership roles should know in advance what is expected of them. Rather than simply having a title, it is important that congregations assign responsibilities to lay leaders that bring some level of accountability. Church consistories or boards are normally comprised of twelve people, and each one should be assigned particular duties. These members are not only accountable to the congregation, but they also stand before the Lord with the promises that they made.

As stated in our section on Christian education, it is essential that congregations focus on the educational needs of their parishioners. Although parishioners may initially resist attending Sunday school or a Bible study, they often reconsider when realizing the benefits. We need knowledgeable and spiritually mature teachers who know how to apply the Scriptures to daily living. The topics that are scheduled should be promoted by the pastor and the education committee. This will help to create an interest in Christian education, maximize the attendance, and provide a recycling effect. There is nothing more exciting than a class that brings the Scriptures into contemporary life. This should be stressed when promoting educational programs. Churches that promote strong educational ministries are a channel for both spiritual and numerical growth.

Pastoral visits may not seem to be a significant factor in community outreach and church growth, but they are part of the total picture. Both church members and new families need personal time with the pastor. Clergy visits enable pastors to know their parishioners in ways not otherwise possible. The relaxed atmosphere of one's residence offers an environment that is conducive to the mutual sharing that brings people together. With few exceptions, people appreciate a pastor's visit because it provides them with an opportunity to express concerns, ask questions, and to share their life story. It also gives people the assurance that their pastor is a true friend, rather than just someone who preaches on Sunday mornings. Whenever possible, these visits should be planned, for it is important that parishioners have time to prepare. Whether the visits are to active members, those who infrequently attend services, or to new visitors, they communicate a person's importance to a congregation.

Another obstacle to church growth involves the acceptance of new people. There are churches that do not live what they proclaim. To be rejected by a Christian congregation is a shocking and painful experience. Regardless of the reason, some churches have a way of alienating people. While these rejections may be subtle, they are nonetheless painful. New people have no desire to be overwhelmed by church members, but they do look for Christian communities that are friendly and accepting. To be a stranger in the Lord's house is devastating and may negatively impact upon a person's spiritual development and concept of the Church. I know Christians who refuse to attend church because of a painful experience. Although I cannot justify this response, I certainly understand their feelings. Just as Jesus died for all sinners, the Church is to welcome everyone regardless where they are in life. The Church is a hospital for the sick, but instead of congregations being places of healing, Christians sometimes slay the wounded in their midst. (Luke 5:31-32) The Lord will never bless a ministry that does not reach out to everyone. Can you imagine if Jesus had rejected the faith and plea of the criminal who was crucified alongside of Him?

Rebuilding a church is a long-term commitment on the part of everyone. The disappointments along the way bring frustration and doubt, but nothing will change if people waver in their efforts and fail to exemplify the teachings of Christ. There is no book or magic wand that brings instant revival to a diminishing congregation. It takes prayer, hard work, and commitment on the part of every person, including children and seniors. My experiences reveal that congregations often seek simplistic solutions to what is a complex problem. Bringing a church back to life is a team effort that takes time.

In one of my parishes, I was faced with a difficult situation. Many of the elderly parishioners could no longer attend worship services and fellowships. They were either homebound or in a nursing facility. Many of the seniors who were attending were also experiencing medical problems that made their attendance sporadic. I officiated at forty funerals during this time, which sent shock waves through the congregation. There were few young families with children, and there was always the possibility of losing them. Along with these challenges was the transiency of a university community.

Having said this, I am pleased to report that after seven years of God's grace and the commitment of remaining members the ministry was revived, and church attendance significantly increased. In fact, an extension was added to the church.

This was also a blessing because it told the community that we were a viable and growing congregation. Before these changes occurred, I shared my concerns with the church consistory. I wanted them to know the obstacles that we faced in rebuilding the congregation. Even though the church had been in the community for 150 years, we were in a situation that wasn't much different from planting a new church.

When parishioners know that they are builders rather than simply members, they see a vision that they desire to embrace. It is not unusual for people to take the initiative by volunteering for particular ministries and other needs. There is normally an increase on all levels of participation, which develops the unity that co-builders need. Also, when parishioners take an active part in the ministry, they begin to invite their family and friends to church. It must be noted that these advances do not occur without strong leadership and the mutual support of the congregation.

The issues relating to community outreach and church growth are many, but this does not mean that some congregations cannot be revived and become a beacon of light in their neighborhoods. If people work together, knowing that change takes time, patience, prayer and commitment, the Holy Spirit will move upon the hearts and lives of people. Revival comes when people have a vision and share in the excitement of ministry. When we are impassioned about something we want others to experience our joy, and this is true of Christian ministry. When churches have a biblical ministry that is pertinent to one's life, people respond with enthusiasm and hope.

SPIRITUAL FORMATION

The Church has the responsibility of communicating sound biblical teachings and doctrine. We also expect congregations to be fellowships that share the love of Jesus Christ. Although these are realistic expectations, the Church has its limitations when it comes to our spiritual growth. Many individuals expect the Church to be the primary source for their spiritual development, which is simply not possible. Even in small churches, pastors are consumed with multiple tasks that limit the time they can give to their parishioners. Clergy are often pulled in so many directions that they can barely accomplish their weekly duties. This is especially true when they are consumed with illnesses and deaths in their parish. These realities emphasize the importance for personal responsibility in developing and sustaining a spiritual life. This must be conveyed to parishioners, encouraging them to study the Scriptures, engage in daily devotions, and to maintain a prayer life.

We cannot blame the Church for what is our responsibility before the Lord. People always find time for entertainment and worldly endeavors, but they resist nurturing their spiritual life. Jesus addressed this neglect when He said, "What good will it be for a man if he gains the world, yet forfeits his soul? Or what will a man give in exchange for his soul?" (Matthew 16:26) Our Savior repeatedly told His followers that they must change their priorities by giving their time and energy to seeking God's kingdom and His righteousness. (Matthew 6:33)

People offer excuses for their lack of spiritual growth, but the Lord knows the heart and mind of every person. During His earthly ministry Jesus was always confronted with people's excuses, and His responses to them were stern. He knew that an excuse is a rejection of the Gospel message and the call to accept His teachings. Rather than being concerned about their spiritual life, many people were only coming to Jesus for physical cures, which is a truth that continues today. While it is not wrong to seek physical healing, it is sad when no thought is given to the inner life and one's salvation. People spend considerable time and money in an attempt to look good, feel good, and to live a long life, but there is little effort given to feed the soul. Unfortunately, those who live this way will reap the painful results.

Everything in life requires time, energy, and commitment, and this includes our spiritual journey. Some people only attend church out of a sense of obligation or to satisfy their conscience. But whether it is at the time of one's death or the Second Advent, everyone will give an account of their life. On the Day of Judgment people will offer excuses for their failure to develop a spiritual life, but the Lord will not be deceived. In the parable of *Lazarus and the Rich Man*, the rich man was sent to hell for his self-centered life and lack of sensitivity to the needs of others. When the rich man offered excuses for his life, Abraham reminded him of the opportunities that he had to make personal changes. (Luke 16:19-31) How can people claim a relationship with God if they lack the desire for spiritual understanding and maturity? Simply professing Christianity and attending a church does not make us disciples. Jesus spoke about this when He said:

> Not everyone who says to me, 'Lord, Lord,' will enter the kingdom of heaven, but only he who does the will of my Father who is in heaven. Many will say to me on that day, 'Lord, Lord, did we not prophesy in your name, and in your name drive out demons and perform many miracles?' Then I will tell them plainly, 'I never knew you. Away from me, you evil doers!' (Matthew 7:21-23)

The parable of the *Four Soils* reveals the varied responses to the Gospel and the teachings of Jesus. The hard soil represents the hard heart that refuses to receive God's Word. The shallow soil over rock is the shallow heart, being those who never develop the roots to sustain a spiritual life. The soil infested with thorns or weeds reflects a life that is overcome with competing interests. All three soils in our Lord's lesson speak to spiritual death. They reveal people's priorities and how they desire to live their lives. Today, they may be church members who refuse to take responsibility for their spiritual development. This is a serious problem that the Church must address in their ministries. While the Church is a gift of grace, it does not replace what God expects of us.

A Christian is one who is transformed through God's grace and personal faith in Jesus Christ. It is living the love and sacrificial life of our Savior. With the past behind us, we become pilgrims on a journey that continuously seeks the heart and mind of Jesus. While perfection in this life is not possible, the sanctifying process enables us to live a life of faith and service to others that is pleasing to God. The apostle Paul said that worship occurs when we offer up our lives as living sacrifices to the Lord. (Romans 12:1) Through our surrender we receive the kingdom of God and the empowering baptism of the Holy Spirit.

As our final chapter will emphasize, the Christian Church is not a building or religious hierarchy, but rather the hearts and souls of people who live in the Spirit. While the institutional Church is God's gift to His people, given for mutual support and spiritual guidance, the true Church lies within every believer. The invisible Church lives and moves through the faith, prayers, and the service of Christians. It is through prayer that spiritual gifts are realized and developed. It is also prayer that provides the strength and direction that is needed for the Church to be a witness in the world. We are called to pray for the universal Church, that all believers might rejoice in their salvation and unite in sharing the good news of Jesus Christ.

It is important that we have realistic expectations of the Church, for even though the Holy Spirit has anointed its mission, secularism and sin will always have its influences. Everyone is aware of the sins that plague the Church, and we have no reason to believe that these problems will end. Realizing the flaws and inconsistencies of the collective Church, we must assume responsibility for our spiritual formation. Our potential in Jesus Christ will never be realized by simply aligning ourselves with the institutional Church. Jesus is in the midst of His people, telling us to focus upon Him and to persistently strive for spiritual maturity. We are in a spiritual battle that will not end until Jesus returns. The apostle Paul was certainly aware of the evil forces that seek our demise. Paul also knew that in Jesus Christ we have the power to be victorious.

— CHAPTER FOUR —

The True Church

WHAT IS THE CHURCH?

God placed all things under his feet and appointed him to be over everything for the Church, which is his body, the fullness of him who fills everything in every way. (Ephesians 1:22-23)

Who is Christ for us today? This question was posed by Dietrich Bonhoeffer, the German theologian and Lutheran pastor who was martyred for opposing Hitler and the Nazi regime. When the Nazi atrocities became known in Germany there were professing Christians who refused to stand firm in the teachings of Jesus Christ. As an institution, the churches in Germany were firmly established, but Bonhoeffer questioned their commitment to the Gospel and Christian values. Like Bonhoeffer, we must question the contemporary Church. What is the life and mission of today's Church? Are we adhering to New Testament teachings and walking in the Spirit? Does politics ever influence our responses to people and situations? Have the teachings of Jesus changed since He called His first disciples?

As a retired pastor, I often find myself framing these questions within the context of my previous ministries. Even when I served as a parish minister and prison chaplain, I frequently analyzed my focus and philosophy of ministry. A pastor's approach to ministry tends to define the dynamics and priorities of a congregation. Other factors include the background and history of a particular church and denomination. But when pondering questions about the Church we should first examine God's involvement with humanity and the teachings of Jesus and the apostles.

As manifested in the Scriptures, God has always been involved with His creation. Prior to the incarnation and ministry of Jesus, the Lord communicated with humanity through natural revelation, the conscience, prophets, the law and sacrifices. His voice was also heard by those whom He chose as leaders of the people. When the people sinned, God spoke through the prophets in an attempt to bring them to repentance and righteous living. Although Israel was set apart to be a sanctified people to serve God and witness to their faith, their failures and sins pointed to the need for a personal Savior, whose love and power would change their hearts and transform their lives. Jesus fulfilled the Hebrew prophecies and the law, bringing God's presence and words directly to those who were searching for truth and desiring to change. Jesus was the Logos, meaning the Word of God, whose death became the one and final sacrifice for all people. In the crucifixion of Jesus, we see both the cost of sin and the perfect love of God. Just as God is the initiator of our salvation, it is His Son who gave us the Church and who rules as its head.

After Pentecost there was an effort by the apostles to organize and plan their ministries. In His commission to them, Jesus said, "All authority in heaven and on earth has been given to me. Therefore, go and make disciples of all nations, baptizing them in the name of the Father, and of the Son, and of the Holy Spirit, and teaching them to obey everything I have commanded you.

And surely, I am with you always, to the end of the age." (Matthew 28:18-20) Although their commission was clear, how did the apostles understand the Church? What did Jesus envision? Was it His intention that financial resources eventually be used to construct buildings? Also, how would Jesus respond to the numerous Christian denominations that exist today? What would He say about their differences? Would our Savior approve of the titles given to clergy? While these questions can be debated, one can assume that our Lord's emphasis was upon people rather than physical structures and hierarchies.

While it is important for Christians to establish locations where they can worship and socialize, the concern relates to the amount of structure that is needed and the cost that is involved. Another factor to examine is how financially dependent denominations are on their local churches. An affiliation with a denomination has benefits, but each congregation needs a level of autonomy in terms of ministries and finances. There has been an increase in non-denominational churches, not simply over scriptural issues, but also because they question supporting large administrations that sometimes seem oblivious to the needs and struggles of congregations.

Leo Tolstoy (1828-1910), was a Russian writer, philosopher and theologian, and a member of the Orthodox Christian Church. In his book *A Confession and Other Religious Writings,* he reveals a struggle with the institutional church of his day. Tolstoy believed that organized religion was disconnected from the realities of the average person. He wrote that the Church lost the Gospel message, which is the law of love that was taught by Christ. Without Jesus being both the focus and head of the Church, there was no consciousness of the Savior's transforming love. As he searched for the simple truths in Christ's teachings, he found an irrelevant church whose dogma and mystery rendered it meaningless.

According to Tolstoy, the Church placed more emphasis upon the ritualistic aspect of the Eucharist than upon the people who Jesus came to save. He also noted that the institutional Church fostered division rather than stressing equality and unity. Tolstoy saw a church that simply went through the motions, was self-serving, and one that failed to internalize and live the teachings of Jesus. He concluded that the majority of members superficially worshipped through habit, a sense of decorum, convenience, fear, and self-interest. Tolstoy called upon the people to free themselves from the superstitions of false Christianity and political structures. While this is not true of many churches, it remains a factor that must be guarded against.

In the Book of Revelation, the apostle John was given the words of the risen Christ concerning seven churches. Some scholars believe that these writings are a literary device or possibly represent seven periods of time. But the explicit content suggests that they were actual churches. It is important that we again emphasize our Savior's words. To the church in Ephesus, Jesus said, "I hold this against you: You have forsaken your first love. Repent, and do the things you did at first. If you do not repent, I will come to you and remove your lamp stand from its place." (Revelation 2:4-5) A church that loses its focus on Jesus and His love will also lose its ministry. Jesus told the people that they must repent and return to where they once were. Failing to do this would result in the removal of their lamp stand, meaning the termination of their ministry.

The Amish maintain a deep sense of spirituality that is realized through simplistic and meaningful forms of worship and service. This is accomplished without the expense of large church buildings, administrative offices, and denominational structures. While they may lack the evangelistic outreach that defines other groups, their faith and focus on Jesus and commitment to one another cannot be questioned. Their witness is found in their lifestyle, which is centered upon God, family, and honest work. In a quiet and selfless way, they reflect the teachings of Christ and Christian values. Like any community, they are not without problems, but they are the Church in every sense of the word.

During my prison chaplaincy, I often thought about the uniqueness of my ministry. I was in a facility of over two thousand inmates, with a Sunday worship attendance that often exceeded three hundred. There were also two weekday Bible studies that were well attended. Our *All Faith Chapel* was a place of refuge and hope for men who were continuously reminded of their failures and crimes. As a closed community, one might assume that spiritual development was limited, and that there was no outreach beyond the prison. But this was not the situation. A significant number of inmates from all the religions dedicated much of their time to studying and understanding their faith. They were on a quest for spiritual knowledge and ministry that would hopefully bring meaning to their imprisonment.

Inmates looked for ways that they could make a difference in society, often contributing their meager incomes to publicized needs, such as the Red Cross and other organizations that receive funds for natural disasters. They were always anxious to communicate their faith to members of society. Within the prison they ministered to those who were going through trials, such as divorce, loss of a loved one, or personal illness. This was done without regard to the other person's beliefs. There were also intercessory prayer groups and Bible studies in the cell blocks. On occasion, they even reached out to staff members who were going through difficult times. In addition, there was an organized ministry that addressed the needs of individuals who were being incarcerated for the first time. They assisted these men with their transition and informed them of spiritual opportunities. Besides these ministries, several times a year our choir went to community churches with a music program. After the worship service they were invited by the congregations to share a meal and fellowship.

Since we were an independent faith group, we did not financially support any outside religious institution. However, we were an active Christian church that followed the teachings of Christ. The inmates reached out through their own pain in an effort to make a difference in the lives of others. This is not to say that there were no issues and challenges. When considering the diversity, emotional struggles, and the stressful environment, education and counseling were essential to maintaining unity and promoting spiritual formation. Like every Christian fellowship, the goal is to unite people in their faith. The following areas are necessary in laying down a strong foundation of love and mission:

- A ministry that is rooted in Jesus Christ
- Making people the priority
- An emphasis upon the forgiving and saving power of the cross

- Teaching the need for a devotional life
- Programs that are specifically aimed at spiritual development and maturity
- Defining leadership, including responsibilities with some manner of follow-up and accountability
- Developing avenues for community outreach that convey the love of Christ
- Create a priesthood of believers who naturally respond to needs

Only when we understand the biblical meaning of the Church will we see other Christians in a positive light, enabling us to celebrate the equality of God's unconditional and infinite love. In the midst of our differences, we are called to unite in the Gospel and in the victory of Christ. This fosters an ecumenical spirit that strengthens the Church and communicates hope in a dark and troubled world. The Church must always be viewed in the broader sense, thus breaking down the barriers that lead to criticism, judgment, conflict division, and isolation. Only God can judge the heart; therefore, we must never judge the salvation of a particular person or group. If there is a concern, it should be a matter of prayer.

CHRISTIAN PARADIGMS

In my ministries I have realized areas that are essential to both personal development and ministry. The objective is to prayerfully allow these models to change us in order that we might reveal Jesus Christ through our lives.

UNITY

The dictionary defines unity as oneness of sentiment, affection and purpose. Paul tells us that we are to live in harmony with one another and be willing to associate with people from all walks of life. (Romans 12:16) The apostle John tells us that people will know who we are through our bond of love. (John 13:34-35; 17:20-23) By the very nature of their faith and new life in Christ, Christians are joined together through the power of the Holy Spirit. Paul's words emphasize that, although many members, we are one body. In his writings he gives the following components of unity:

- One body and one Spirit (Ephesians 4:4; Romans 12:5; I Corinthians 12:27)
- Called to one hope (Ephesians 4:4; Romans 15:4)
- One Lord, one faith, one baptism (Ephesians 4:5; I Timothy 2:5)
- One God and Father of all, who is over all, and through all, and in all (Ephesians 4:6; I Corinthians 12:4-6; 15:24-28)

Christian unity has its beginning in the oneness of the Triune God, who emptied Himself to bring life to fallen humanity. Through the incarnation, Jesus united with us, experiencing our burdens and trials. The wounds of our Savior forever communicate the cost of our unity and the inclusion for which Jesus suffered. Christ died for all people that we might become one in faith, mission and hope. We are called from every nation to serve God and one another in the love of Christ. Christians are to serve and be served without the thought of boundaries.

As Jesus completed His work, even as He faced death, He contemplated the lives of His disciples. He was concerned about the unity of His followers, wanting them to be united in love and purpose. The Scriptures tell us that He fervently prayed for that unity. (John 13:14; 17:21) In their tumultuous world, the disciples were called to be one body that others might know God's forgiving and saving grace. For our witness to be strong it must be manifested as an undivided whole that is void of division and conflict. This means that we must continuously strive for divine love and an ecumenical spirit. It is amazing how some people claim to have the love of Christ, yet they are continuously at war with one another.

Only through the inner Spirit will distinctions and differences lose their power, thus making all Christians humble and joyful servants who rejoice in their Savior's mercy. This is a powerful truth when considering the things that divide us. The first-century Church would not have survived the persecutions, diversity, transitions, and the environmental tensions, without the inner Spirit. Luke tells us that regardless of their differences, early Christians somehow had all things in common. (Acts 2:42-47) The fellowship of the Spirit affirms differences, except when they are used in oppressive and dehumanizing ways.

The diversity of my prison congregation was extreme. At the one end of the spectrum were Episcopalians who saw reverence in silent reflection, liturgy, and orderly worship. In comparison, were Pentecostal inmates who were vocal, spontaneous, and animate in their worship. We also had individuals from various denominations, as well as those who had no spiritual background. Also, many of the men had strong and controlling personalities that presented challenges. But regardless of these dynamics we had a congregation that united in faith. This was accomplished through a continuous emphasis upon Christian unity, a topic that was integrated into prayers, biblical lessons, preaching and worship. Midweek Bible studies also emphasized biblical teachings on unity. I came to realize that this subject must be stressed in every ministry, with an emphasis upon the positive aspects of diversity. It is diversity that reflects God's creativity and serves as an avenue for objective learning and personal development.

Christians do not need to be carbon copies of one another. Even the members of one's household have different perceptions and ideas about their faith. In fact, differences must be expected. I am certain that one day we will all undergo personal and theological transformations. What is important on this side of eternity is that we love and encourage everyone. When a particular church believes that they have all the answers, to the exclusion of other believers, the result is division within the body of Christ. This weakens the witness of the universal Church. Ecumenism is not simply a word, but rather an essential truth that must begin within each person and taught in every congregation. The bond that unites every Christian is the one Savior who gave His life for humanity. The foundation of the Church can only remain strong when its members unite under the banner of Jesus Christ.

Rather than being separatists, clergy should encourage worship services with churches of other denominations. This creates an understanding and objectivity that eliminates suspicion and judgment. My first parish was initially opposed to this, but after some lengthy conversations they agreed to have our Good Friday service with another church. The results were quite surprising!

Everyone who worshipped attested to the blessings that they received. We had a combined choir, and I shared the pulpit with the other pastor. After the worship service we had a time of fellowship that was full of conversation and laughter. Our folks even learned that many of the parishioners in the other church were neighbors and co-workers. This tradition continued, with the number of joint services increasing. The members of both churches began to realize the vastness of God's kingdom and the grace that flows through all Christian churches.

Although Christians may differ in their understanding and approach to Holy Communion, the sacrament expresses the unity that we share in Jesus Christ. When we partake of the elements, we acknowledge that we are all in need of God's forgiveness and grace. No one is worthy of salvation apart from the grace that flows through Jesus Christ. Clergy should stress this truth when administering the sacrament. We come before the Lord stripped of ethnicity, race, socioeconomic standing and good works. All that matters is our humility, repentant heart and faith. Our secular accomplishments are only recognized within the context of God's calling and plan for our lives. We come before the Lord as equals, who are equally loved by our Creator. Mother Teresa said that at the time of death we are all equal. This is a penetrating truth! Each time we receive the sacrament we are reminded of our dependency and equality before God.

After leaving the prison system I served a small parish that desperately needed young families who would be the future of our congregation. In an attempt to build a foundation for the next generation I decided to teach a catechism class. In addition to our denominational material, I wanted our young folks to understand the need for Christian unity. I also thought that it was important to introduce them to the other monotheistic religions. To accomplish this, I first explained the essential beliefs of those faiths. Arrangements were then made to worship in those settings and for the students to receive insights from a rabbi, imam, and Roman Catholic priest. The intention was to emphasize our commonality with these faith groups and to develop an appreciation for their history and traditions. In essence, it was to expose the students to the broader picture of God's revelations and His involvement with humanity. This was a lesson on unity and how people of all faiths are on a journey for truth.

In the first century the Gospel was preached to people from all walks of life, and diversity was certainly an issue. Even the apostles and early followers had their differences. (Acts 15) But these differences were overcome when the focus was upon the saving grace that comes through faith in Jesus Christ. In spite of differences, their essential beliefs built a foundation for the universal Church. Paul's epistles reveal the growing pains of the churches, but their faith and apostolic leadership gave them victory. These are important lessons for us to remember.

PRIESTHOOD OF BELIEVERS

On Mount Sinai, God told His people that they would be a priestly kingdom and a holy nation. (Exodus 19:6) This proclamation seems to relate to individuals who would be religious leaders and intercessors for Israel, but the prophet Joel spoke about a day when all of God's people would receive the Holy Spirit, which would create a priesthood for mutual ministry. In fulfillment of this prophecy the Holy Spirit has been poured out upon all believers, granting them gifts for serving one another.

Paul told Christians to rid themselves of pride and to carry one another's burdens. (Galatians 6:2) He wanted them to pray for one another and to provide encouragement and support that would not otherwise be possible. We are the keepers of our brothers and sisters, offering strength to the weak, love to the loveless, and hope to those living in despair. Because the Lord meets our needs, we in turn are impelled by the Spirit to meet the needs of others. Our mission is not only to help people with their physical and emotional pain, but to also lead them to the *Great Physician* for their spiritual needs. Although the priesthood primarily speaks to mutual ministry within a congregation, it certainly extends outside the Christian community. We are God's covenant partners; therefore, we do not live in isolation. Jesus is wholly the *Good Samaritan* whose example demands that we follow, moving beyond the barriers that block compassion and mercy.

While the clergy typically assume priestly positions, they are limited in what they can do. It is important, therefore, that church leaders promote a priesthood within their faith groups. Many people have difficulty understanding how they can minister to others, but all Christians are called by God to make a difference. We not only possess the gift of love, but the Lord has granted other gifts that need to be developed. When I was studying for the ministry the mere thought of speaking or preaching before a congregation was overwhelming. However, I stepped out in faith, believing that the Lord was leading me into the ministry. When looking back I can now see how God was working in my life, progressively increasing my confidence.

The priesthood is a ceaseless ministry that builds God's earthly kingdom through compassion and acts of mercy. An active priesthood results in the following benefits and spiritual gifts:

- Creates objectivity and understanding of human diversity
- Realizes the meaning and power of God's love
- Eliminates self-absorption
- Discovers and develops gifts for both personal growth and ministry to others
- Teaches humility and the importance of being a servant
- Builds the faith and inner strength needed for evangelistic outreach
- Creates sensitivity, tolerance, and the acceptance of others
- Brings meaning and purpose to one's life
- Receives the multiple blessings that come through serving others
- Brings us closer to the Lord

The prophet Isaiah revealed that the Messiah would come as a humble servant with a gentle spirit. He wrote, "He will not shout or cry out, or raise his voice in the streets. A bruised reed he will not break, and a smoldering wick he will not snuff out. In faithfulness he will bring forth justice." (Isaiah 42:2-3) Jesus rejected any notion of worldly power, status or privilege. His presence was one of compassion and healing in which others came first. He cured the lepers, washed the feet of His disciples, called children to His side, encouraged women and, in the end, He willingly submitted to crucifixion. Jesus came not only to proclaim the coming of God's kingdom, but He gave His life to open God's realm and presence to everyone.

The priesthood is the presence of Christ in action. Jesus entered our world as a humble and self-less servant to share our burdens and to carry our sins. Like Jesus, we are to serve others in His spirit of love. When this is realized, everyone becomes a recipient of divine grace. Our Savior teaches us that true love is radical and has no boundaries. We love and serve others because the love of Christ is in us. In other words, it is a natural response to the needs around us. Those who live only for themselves will lose eternal life. Jesus said to His disciples, "Anyone who does not take up his cross and follow me is not worthy of me. Whoever finds his life will lose it, and whoever loses his life for my sake will find it." (Matthew 10:38-39) To be bound to God is to be bound to those in need. Dietrich Bonhoeffer's representation of Jesus as *The Man for Others* expresses our calling, for the servant is no greater than the *Master*. Any church or ministry that does not emphasize serving others is not walking in the footsteps of Christ.

MINISTRY OF PRESENCE

The ministry of presence is the priesthood being extended into our daily living. Whether it is a smile, kind words or good deeds, it is a Christ-like presence that makes a difference in the world. Before His ascension Jesus told His apostles that His presence would always be with them. When He gave them their commission, He said, "*Teach them to obey everything I have commanded you. And surely, I am with you always, to the very end of the age."* (Matthew 28:20) Jesus also said, *"In this world you will have trouble. But take heart! I have overcome the world."* (John 16:33) Likewise, the apostle John wrote, *"You, dear children are from God and have overcome them, because the one who is in you is greater than the one who is in the world."* (I John 4:4) God has never forsaken the humanity that He created. Even when Israel was rebellious and courting sin, the Lord was speaking to them through the prophets. Throughout biblical history we see God reaching out to the people.

Although our sins have had destructive effects, God continuously desires our love and service in His kingdom. Those who are reconciled are called to be servants of mercy. As the salt of the earth, our presence is needed to bring healing to a dying world. The Church is not only a moral presence, but also one that restores humanity. Although Christians remain imperfect, their presence is a beacon of spiritual light and hope. Just as Paul needed God's presence to fight unseen forces, the world needs the movement of the Holy Spirit to transform the hearts of people. The Church is a presence that meets people where they are in life, offering encouragement, strength, and the promises of Christ. Christians are servants of mercy who reach out to those who are engaged in struggles of the mind, body and spirit. The true Church is a hospital that tends to the sick, which includes those whom society deems incurable. Our Savior's words accentuate how important our presence is to those who are in need:

> *Jesus said, "I was hungry and you gave me something to eat, I was thirsty and you gave me something to drink, I was a stranger and you invited me in, I needed clothes and*

you clothed me. I was sick and you looked after me, I was in prison and you came to visit me. I tell you the truth, whatever you did for one of the least of these brothers of mine, you did for me." (Matthew 25:35, 36, 40)

The ministry of presence is sharing in both the joys and struggles of humanity. It is being joyful with the joyful, weak with the weak, vulnerable with the vulnerable, and sad with those who are walking in pain. It is an unconditional love that responds through the Spirit who lives within us, moving beyond our structures to identify with one's life situation. Like the *Good Samaritan,* our concern is only for the person and the alleviation of their suffering and hopelessness. It is a presence without ulterior motives and seeks nothing in return. Because we are one with our Savior our response is natural and without hesitation. Love only becomes a reality when it is given away, and this translates into concrete acts of compassion.

Jesus reminds us that ministry to the least is ministry to Him. When we minister to those in need, we become one with Him in His burden and compassion for humanity. As the body of Christ, we are the extension and continuation of Jesus and His ministry in this dark world. Like Jesus, we must penetrate the walls of separation that are caused by prejudice, mistrust, anger and fear. This is not our natural response, and there is a tendency to remove ourselves from such discomfort. But as His disciples, Jesus sends us into the same places where the Father sent Him. It is not our calling to condemn or demand to know the reasons for a person's situation. Instead, it is only to administer God's love.

Our presence can be summed up in the word *compassion.* Jesus had compassion for the people because they were like sheep without a shepherd. (Mark 6:34) They were lost, walking around in darkness, and they could not find their way to the mercy and grace that God was offering. They needed a Savior to open their hearts and lead them to the kingdom of God. This is our mission; therefore, we must be alert to the leading of the Holy Spirit and the burdens that God places upon our hearts. Jesus identifies with us through the suffering that He endured, and this same avenue speaks to us concerning other people. We often identify with the pain of others because we have experienced pain. Whether it is divorce, losing a loved one, illness or financial stress, Christians touch the lives of others through their own wounds. Henri Nouwen's book *The Wounded Healer*, provides enlightening insights into this aspect of ministry. Paul believed that our experiences, combined with a Christ-like presence, not only brings comfort and healing to individuals, but it is also a vehicle to lead people to Christ. Jesus came to us as a *suffering servant* with words and acts of love, and this is what draws us to Him. Only love speaks to the heart and awakens human emotion and spiritual desires.

Prison chaplains walk a fine line when interacting with inmates. Unlike a local parish, security is the primary concern in penal institutions. This fact must always take precedence, even when clergy believe that the Gospel is overshadowed by regulations. While security issues may at times hamper the ministry, they should always be confronted in the spirit of love. We must always be an understanding and compassionate presence, even in the most difficult situations. Prisoners know the rules, but they expect them to be enforced in a manner that conveys respect. I learned that you can say *no* to people, but you can do it in love and in a way that offers explanations and alternatives. Chaplains may not be able to change a prisoner's situation, but they can be a presence of understanding and compassion that can change an inmate's heart. This is the approach that must guide everyone, regardless of the situation.

While at the prison I learned the importance of the ministry of presence. It was my routine to visit cell blocks, the exercise yard, dispensary, and solitary confinement. These visits made a difference in the lives of the inmates. In some cases, it was all that they had to look forward to each day. The inmates knew that, when all else failed, they could share their difficulties with a compassionate and helpful presence. What amazed me, is the joy and peace that prisoners feel when they are in the presence of Christians. The ministry of presence is sharing the other person's burdens. It is prayerfully entering their emotional world, knowing that the identification and bonding will bring peace to their troubled spirit. As the *Suffering Servant*, Jesus was moved by what He encountered during His ministry, and He was quick to respond. Regardless of the situation, He knew that whatever distorted God's intention for humanity was a destructive force. He was a presence that placed humanity above all else. There was nothing in His nature or life that was self-serving. What a lesson for us!

Jesus socialized with the wealthy, the poor, and with the worst of sinners. He came face to face with all manner of sickness, disease, and manifestations of evil. His life was one of both words and action, thereby setting the example for those who would pick up their cross and follow Him. He was all things to all people, considering the needs and uniqueness of every person that He encountered on His earthly journey. He willingly accepted His crucifixion as God's will, being the path that would bring salvation to countless people.

His mission was one of urgency, knowing that opportunities do not last. He said to His disciples, "As long as it is day, we must do the work of him who sent me. Night is coming when no one can work. While I am in the world, I am the light of the world." (John 9:4-5) Jesus knew that His presence would change the lives of those who received Him and lived by His teachings.

Our Savior was not only a compassionate presence to others, but He also sought compassion Himself. When He was in the Garden of Gethsemane, He felt the weight of the suffering that He would soon endure. In His pain, He asked His disciples to stay awake with Him. Even though the disciples could not prevent the chain of events that were about to take place, Jesus wanted the comfort of their presence. Little did the disciples know how important it was for them to be there with Jesus before He was arrested. (Matthew 26:36-46) Although the Son of God, He lived in the flesh and experienced all the emotions that are common to us.

Jesus did not heal everyone that He came in contact with, nor did He solve all of their problems. But He did reinforce their importance and give them hope. Although He confronted sin, He did not condemn people. Instead, He offered them forgiveness and a new way of life. He knew that once they received Him into their hearts that the Holy Spirit would enter their lives and be their guide. Learning this lesson would serve us well, for too often we judge others and block the movement of the Holy Spirit. Our mission is to continue the unconditional love that was manifested in our Savior's life and sacrificial death. God has called us to be healers in a broken world that is in the grip of sin. Only love can bring people to Jesus Christ; the same love that led us to forgiveness and reconciliation with God.

Our Lord never spoke about worldly structures or denominations when alluding to His Church. Jesus' focus and, that of His apostles, is that we develop a spiritual life and serve humanity. Having said this, it is important that everyone find a faith group that preaches the Gospel, promotes biblical education and understanding, and one that has an outreach into the community. Apart from a Christian fellowship, few people have the discipline to mature in their faith or be directed and encouraged to be ministers to others.

It must again be emphasized that, while there are many parts in the body of Christ, there is one Savior who is the head of the Church. There is no individual, group or denomination that takes the place of our Savior's position over the Church. This means that we must always pray for understanding and divine guidance. Knowing that Christ is the head of the Church, the apostles always prayed for God's presence, intercession and leading. This is a valuable truth to guide us.

Resources

Board of Publication, Lutheran Church in America. *Service Book and Hymnal.* Minneapolis: Augsburg Publishing House, 1958-75.

Bonhoeffer, Dietrich. *The Cost of Discipleship.* New York: Macmillan Publishing Company, 1963.

Deal, William S. *Baker's Pictorial Introduction to the Bible*: Grand Rapids: Baker Book House Company, 1967.

Eiselen, Frederick; Lewis, Edwin; Downey, David G., editors. *The Abingdon Bible Commentary.* New York: Abingdon Press, 1929.

Fischer, Louis. *The Life of Mahatma Gandhi.* New York: Harper and Row Publishers, 1950.

Gore, Charles, editor. *A New Commentary on Holy Scriptures: Including the Apocrypha.* New York: MacMillan Co., 1928.

Haines, Lee. *The Wesleyan Bible Commentary, Volume 1, Part 1: Genesis-Deuteronomy.* Grand Rapids: Baker House, 1960.

Hanke, Howard A. *The Wesleyan Bible Commentary – Numbers and Deuteronomy.* Grand Rapids: William B. Eerdmans Publishing Company, 1967.

Harrison, Everett F. *Dictionary of Theology.* Grand Rapids: Baker House, 1960.

His Holiness John Paul II. *Crossing the Threshold of Hope.* New York: Alfred A. Knopf, Inc., 1994.

Holy Bible - New International Version. Grand Rapids: Zondervan Corporation, 1978.

Jones, Kenneth E. *The Wesleyan Bible Commentary, Volume III: Isaiah-Malachi.* Grand Rapids: William B. Eerdmans Publishing Co., 1969.

Kauffman, Donald T. *The Dictionary of Religious Terms.* New Jersey: Fleming H. Revell Company, 1967.

Martinez, Luis M. *Only Jesus.* United States of America: B. Herder Book Company, 1962.

Nave, Orville J., ed. *Nave's Topical Bible.* Milford: Mott Media, Inc., 1984.

Nouwen, Henri J. M. *The Way of the Heart.* New York: Ballantine Books, 1981.

Ridderbos, Herman. *Paul, An Outline of His Theology.* Grand Rapids: William B. Eerdmans Publishing Company, 1975.

Rushdoony, John. *The Institutes of Biblical Law.* United States: The Presbyterian and Reformed Publishing Company and Craig Press, 1973.

Smith, William. *Smith's Bible Dictionary.* Philadelphia: A.J. Holman and Company, 1980.

Tasker, R.V. G., ed. *The Epistle of Paul to the Galatians.* Grand Rapids: William B. Eerdmans Publishing Company, 1965,1977.

Tillich, Paul. *The Eternal Now.* New York: Scribner's Sons, 1963.

Unger, Merrill F. *Unger's Bible Dictionary.* Chicago: Moody Press, 1957-87.

Whiston, William – paraphrase of his edition. *Josephus: Thrones of Blood.* Uhrichsville, Ohio: Barbour and Company, Inc., 1988.

Young, Robert. *Young's Analytical Concordance to the Bible.* Grand Rapids: William B. Eerdmans Publishing Company, 1964.

MORE BY DR. HENRY G. COVERT

Journey to the Next World: Understanding Death & Resurrection
Death and the afterlife speak to everyone. Dr. Covert examines our life journey from different perspectives, including the biblical understanding of death and resurrection and the events leading to the Second Advent of Jesus. He reminds us of the many obstacles and destructive forces that are encountered as we journey to our heavenly home. The reader is urged to make preparation by nourishing the inner life with the gifts of the Holy Spirit. This book is educational, spiritually motivating, and encouraging.
(139pp. Masthof Press, 2022.) $12.00

Ministry to the Incarcerated
Dr. Covert uses his experiences as both police officer and state prison chaplain to examine the environment of the incarcerated—people who are often forgotten by society. He emphasizes particular areas of inmate stress and how they impact upon the inmate's spiritual formation and the role of the Church in offering encouragement, healing and transformation. He calls for staff education, environmental improvement, and a pastoral presence that facilitates rehabilitation and hope, rather than discouragement and punishment.
(185pp. index. Masthof Press, 2022) $12.00

Prayers That God Hears
The misconceptions relating to prayer make it a topic that is often abstract and difficult to understand. Dr. Covert's treatment of the subject is both biblically rooted and realistic. The simplicity of this book brings a clarity and continuity that is easily grasped and applied to one's life. It answers our questions and speaks to our deepest needs and struggles. This book is for everyone who seeks a meaningful relationship with God and others.
(140pp. Masthof Press, 2022) $12.00

www.ingramcontent.com/pod-product-compliance
Lightning Source LLC
Chambersburg PA
CBHW070100080526
44586CB00013B/1136